I0406812

Presence

A TAPESTRY OF LOVE

THROUGH THE EYES OF THE SOUL

Joyce Swann Gedeon

ISBN-13:

978-1466413139

ISBN-10:

1466413131

Order at joycegedeon.com

Publishing services by Utopihost.com

Edited by Pat Smith

This book is dedicated to:

My late husband – Peter Jay Gedeon

Spiritual Guide and light being – Jubal

Special thanks and much love to:

The many Guides and Guardian Angels on the other side

who guided the words on these pages.

Friends and teachers Betty, now Beatrice, Mary Reed, Geoffrey and

Diana Bullington.

Phyllis A. Whitney who mentored me in my writing

and gave me the encouragement to keep writing.

Sandra Solomon who gave support and insight everyday as I wrote.

All of the people mentioned in this book who were part of the

tapestry.

My son, Jonathan Gedeon, who accepted and emotionally supported

his unusual mother,

and my son, Peter Michael Gedeon, who helped

despite my resistance, bring me into the computer age, designed the

cover, and got this book out to the world.

Forward

If one got caught up in the illusion of the third dimension, it may seem an impossible task to interpret the seemingly mystical yet pretty ordinary happenings of my life. Fortunately, I have been blessed with a unique insight – some may call it holographic – not linear but inter-dimensional. This book was written from that perspective. Since we live at this moment, in our physical bodies, in the third dimension of time and space, presenting this material to you is at times challenging. It is that very challenge that draws me to this project.

Creating has always been my passion. At a very early age I knew I was destined to be an artist. I went to art school and for many years, I saw myself as a sculptor and art teacher. What that meant, in my then limited linear world, turned out to be very different from what I now understand.

As the tapestry of my life has been woven, I have developed the perspective that in a way we have all been students in a universal art school. Upon graduation we are given back our free will. If we choose we no longer have to be slaves to the karmic wheel that we have been continually experiencing in this dimension. All of the lifetimes of lessons that make up our tapestries are coming to a state of completion now. This new consciousness is birthing a new wave of creation. As souls we may now choose to be co-creators, divine artists, creating divine order and universal oneness.

To create our tapestry we have been given the greatest of all tools ever created – *love*. It is with this tool that I weave these pages. It is in this stream of thought that I come to *you* to reconnect with your unique creative energy field. It is in this creative energy field of union and love that all is possible. Our journey into the reality of the other dimensions is merged in this dimension and anchored onto the planet through our physical vehicles. Through the awakening of the eternal union with Source, we are at one with all.

One may also say that as we shed our limited perspectives of who we thought we were, and put on the new mantel of our god selves, the illusion of being alone disappears as we step into the reality that we were never separate from God. We, as a collective consciousness, are God creating – creating heaven on earth in full remembrance and awakening. Now we may be awakened, once again, seeing through the eyes of the soul.

It is with this understanding of the Universal Truth that I write this book. As this page is being created by this universal collective consciousness, the words unfold to reveal an inter-dimensional journey. My desire is to share this journey, knowing that if you chose, it may assist you. It is my prayer that it may create a reawakening and inner knowing, that may not make much sense in the linear three dimensional world, but in your heart it is easily understood.

Some of the passages are italicized. As I write, them my awareness leaves this dimension, so that an expanded connection to the Universal Truth can come through. Some people call this channeling. Since nothing is separate, one has no need to go outside of self to bring the words through. One may equate it to turning a dial in the brain to a different frequency to pick up the appropriate messages from within.

Each soul has this same knowledge and ability within them. It is not unique to only a few special souls. All souls are equal. Within the purity of the soul there is no ego. One need only have faith and love of self to awaken to this ability.

The stories that are shared are about an ordinary soul having extraordinary adventures in creation. These true stories are shared to be a bridge that may carry our awareness back to the *I AM* of being.

The tapestry is a metaphor – a bridging mechanism. When one exists in the third dimension of linear time, you find yourself enmeshed in the weave of the story that is unfolding. As you become the weaver, you remember that the stories and events in the tapestry are not separate but a part of the whole design.

The view point of the weaver then becomes holographic. You may now see what has been done and at the same time the work that is in progress – the past and present. You may use this perspective to envision new possibilities for future blue prints of personal creation.

Even though the threads are still being woven in the moment, the inter- dimensional weaver sees the whole tapestry as it has always been designed. That design is the master plan – divine plan. How the threads are woven is in progress but the final result serves the whole. Every thread or event supports every other thread or event.

We have come from being the thread in the creation to being the weaver of the creation. I ask you now to visualize yourself as just one weaver in a huge factory of weavers, all working together to create a huge tapestry. Then go one step above and see a town made up of factories all having the same job, to create a tapestry that will be sent to the capital of the country. Like a puzzle coming together, all the pieces combine to form one creation – one tapestry. See each country of the world and all life as weavers of their own creation that then go out to be interwoven. Then see unfolding a global tapestry; revealing a planet surrounded by one creation with not one thread separate from the whole.

The planet rejoices as its purpose appears to be fulfilled. Then, yet another weaver comes in to join the earth's global tapestry with all the tapestries that have ever been created. This weaver is a universal traveler joining our tapestry with that of moons, stars, planets, universes, other galaxies, and dimensions together. As above so below – infinitely in and infinitely out – the macro and the micro – all threads of the universal tapestry are now connected together by *love*.

It doesn't matter which you choose to be in the moment, a weaver, a thread, one tiny atom, or an immense galaxy. All is perfect and equal in the creator's eyes. It is each thread that creates the whole – the creator. The tapestry is already completed. We are just weaving the final threads to tie it all together once again with *love*.

It is sometimes difficult to remember the whole when we are focused on the illusion of separateness. To walk our talk and live together as one knowing that we were never separate from the source of all creation. We doubt that we ever had a purpose for existing, when we lose sight in the illusion, of our value in the greater scheme of things. This doubt is just another part of the creation, it helps define *faith* and *purpose*. Without the darkness or fear in the design, the love and light would not seem as clear and bright. The contrasting colors and different degrees of light make the tapestry richer. All has purpose.

As you read this book, I invite you to consciously weave your tapestry into mine, relating the experiences of your own unique life. It is then that together we remember the union of the oneness and the power of God – within and without.

Sit back and let go. Give to your God Self – your soul – all doubts, fears, and confusion. Remember, above all else, have fun. Enjoy this wondrous journey you are about to embark on with all of creation. You may view it as you would a Steven Spielberg movie with a lot of special effects and a plot that even Steven hasn't conceived of yet – the everyday life of an inter-dimensional women living at the dawn of a new millennium.

Introduction

One might say I have multiple personalities. That's not the case but it comes close to describing the truth. Unless you have ever been a vessel for the other worlds, it may be difficult to fully understand exactly what it is like. Words somehow aren't quite adequate to express what really occurs. Many people have different views, explanations, or beliefs about the process of channeling. I like to think that when information is given to me it is coming from my soul which has never been separate from God – all creation. Within the I AM of my soul, all knowledge of Universal Truth and communication with all aspects of creation are possible.

We know that scientists explore subatomic worlds with microscopes. They have discovered worlds we can not see with the physical eye. Why then, is it so difficult to believe that other worlds might also exist in the same space; spirit worlds, which are not in our scope of vision with these third dimensional eyes?

I have had so many experiences that could not be explained to me logically that I have been left with no doubt as to the existence of other worlds or dimensions within this one. I don't believe I am unique. I just see through a different awareness. I have learned to see through the eyes of the soul. My life experiences have taught me how to do this.

When seen through the eyes of the soul, what would appear

to be a miracle is merely an everyday event. The impossible is expected, and the unexpected predictable. The soul knows all, sees all, and is part of all.

Chapter 1

We will now go on a journey through the eyes of my soul to one of the earliest memories I have in this incarnation. We journey to four years of age. It was winter; my brother, Wayne, was just a baby and sleeping in a crib next to me. That day my father and I had built an incredible snow sculpture in the front yard. It was a reclining lion. My father, who was very artistic, wasn't happy just building a regular snowman, although we made one of those too. I remember how regal and powerful the lion looked. Standing next to the lion was Frosty the Snowman. We used black stones for eyes and a carrot for a nose. I gave him my scarf to keep him warm and my father put a broom in his hand. My imagination could pretend that he might come to life just like Frosty the Snowman did in the book.

At night, like many children, I was fearful of the dark and open closet doors, where my vivid imagination, as some called it, pictured all sorts of things lurking in the shadows. On this night the things I experienced were not just imagined and no one could ever tell me any different.

As I lay in bed strange colors swirled in the room. Things seemed to move. And as usual I couldn't get to sleep. At night when the lights went out for everyone else they seemed to come on for me. I had no understanding of the things I saw in what should have been darkness, and great fear consumed me almost every night. Every inch of me was under the covers which I had tightly tucked in under my body, so I wouldn't float away or be touched by the shapes that I couldn't explain. The only things exposed to the air were my nose and eyes.

I thought of the snowman and the lion and the fun I had with my daddy that day and finally dozed off to sleep as my eyelids grew too heavy to keep open. In the middle of the night I was suddenly awakened. There, standing next to my bed, was a fuzzy white glowing figure. Our snowman, I thought, had come to be with me. At least for the moment that's how my mind explained the figure who was looking down at me. At first I wasn't afraid, just curious. I lay for a while looking at him and then my logical mind took over. How could a snowman stand for so long in a warm house and not melt? He didn't appear to be melting.

As my inability to explain this being who was looking at me grew so did my fear. Suddenly my curiosity became panic. I screamed out loudly and forcefully, "Mom, come quick; there's a snowman in my room and he's not melting!" Because I was so upset my parents allowed me to get into bed with them. (This was something that rarely occurred.) The next day the neighbor asked my mother what had happened the night before. Apparently my screams had been so loud that they could be heard two doors down the street. My mother explained that it was just a nightmare. No one believed me. I knew it wasn't a nightmare. This event was etched so deeply in my memory that I never forgot it. It wasn't until many years later that I found out why it was so important.

It's difficult for me to believe that it's been over 17 years since my husband made his transition suddenly in a plane crash. Though most of the tears have finally stopped, my fond loving memories of him will never leave. When my world suddenly came crashing down around me, I turned to the other invisible worlds for comfort – the worlds I had known as a young child when I lay in bed at night watching the ceiling that appeared to move and change color as I left my body to journey. The memory that there was more than just this physical world returned and my connection to those other worlds began again.

Pete was now in another world and every part of me longed to be with him. I was living in a small town with no family around me and at the time unemployed. I was very pregnant and the sole support of a three year old. I had no fear of lack and felt totally supported by Spirit, the invisible forces that had always been with me from early childhood. Many around me wondered how I found the strength to go on. They weren't aware of my strong faith and reasons for having it.

My husband, Pete, had been working as curator of the Maritime Museum in St. Michaels We had a three year old son named Jonathan, and lived in a small house just outside town. I was a stay-at-home mom and our bills exceeded our income. We were just keeping our heads above water but the three of us were very happy. My husband loved his job and I loved him and my son. Life seemed simple and almost perfect.

One summer day after Pete and I had gone to lunch in town,

we walked across what is called the Kissing Bridge which looks out over the harbor of St. Michaels. We held hands and we were enjoying a wonderful afternoon together. Pete told me about a man with a sea plane who kept asking him to go flying with him. From time to time my husband went up with another pilot to take aerial photographs for the museum. Pete was an artist and loved photography. He had no desire to fly with this person but the man wouldn't stop asking him to go. As he told me about this man a cold, empty feeling came over me. I felt very sad and lonely as we stood together on the small bridge looking out over the harbor. I held his hand, looked into his eyes, and pleaded with him not to fly with this man. I told him, "I can't explain why, I just have a feeling something horrible might happen if you go up with him. I know you probably won't listen to me but I have to warn you not to go with him."

Pete smiled and said, "Don't worry, I have no desire to fly with him. I have been doing my best to avoid him."

That fall Pete had been asked to do some photos over again for a brochure for the museum. He had taken some shots earlier but they wanted him to get closer views of various parts of the museum. They were in a hurry for the pictures. The woman pilot he usually flew with was busy and the man I had warned him about was the only one available that day. This pilot was eager to show off his flying and his new sea plane. The museum staff was insisting he go to get the job done.

It was a very calm day and the waters of the Miles River were glassy and mirror- like. The seaplane was seen making touch down landings and taking off in the harbor and surrounding area. The pilot was even seen doing figure eights in the water at high speeds. Normally it is extremely dangerous to fly in this manner, but on a calm day the surface of the water can be illusionary and even more dangerous. One can misjudge the true surface of the water and that is what we believe happened. What the pilot thought was the surface was really the bottom of the river bed. Misjudging the surface the pilot flew the plane directly into the water.

The plane was totally destroyed. The pilot survived with some injuries. Pete was thrown out of his failed seat belt, through the propeller, and then into the water. He was picked out of the water by some watermen in a boat which happened to be near by when the plane crashed into the river. A helicopter took him to a shock trauma center in Baltimore. I just missed the helicopter and had to be driven to the hospital hours away.

The news came to me as I was sitting in my rocking chair with my three year old son. It was nap time and I was attempting to get Jon, who never did like naps, to go to sleep. There was a knock on my door. It was a neighbor who worked for the harbor patrol.

As I stood in the doorway looking at this man in uniform wondering what he could possibly want with me, he said, "Mrs. Gedeon your husband has been in an accident."

I said, "You must be mistaken my husband is at work. You must have the wrong person. In fact my husband is due home any minute now."

He kept insisting, "No Mrs. Gedeon. I am sure it was your husband. There has been a plane crash and they are taking him to a shock trauma hospital in Baltimore. If you want I will take you to him."

There was a sinking feeling in the pit of my stomach. Even though I didn't want to accept it I finally started to believe what he was saying. I took my son to the neighbor's house and went with the man in uniform to try to catch the helicopter before it took off for the hospital.

I was totally caught up in the drama. The man was telling me that Pete's arm was severed and crews were trying to recover it in hopes it could be put back on. All this seemed too unbelievable to be true. Just a moment before everything was perfect and now I found myself in a very real nightmare. All I could think about was the hope they could find his arm. I couldn't bear to think of Pete – my talented husband – without his right arm. I couldn't allow myself to focus on anything else for fear things could be even worse.

We raced into town and down one of the narrow streets that lead to the harbor very near that Kissing Bridge where I had that empty feeling just months before – the same empty feeling I now had in the pit of my stomach. The helicopter was just taking off. I jumped out of the car and ran down the street, my arms stretched high above my head. The sound of the helicopter was so loud it seemed to vibrate through every part of me. I screamed, "Come back, Come back!" but it seemed no one heard. I felt totally alone on my own private island even though I was in the middle of a whole crowd of people that had gathered. It seemed they didn't even know that I was there. The strong wind from the prop tried to dry my tears but that task was impossible.

As the helicopter climbed higher and higher in the sky, I wished I could leave my body as I had when I was a small child and go with it.

I stood there in the middle of the street not able to move and not able to lower my arms. One of the rescue workers recognized me. She came to me and said, "I was with your husband before the helicopter arrived. The good news is your husband never lost consciousness. His main concern was not for himself but for you. He mentioned you many times. He was alert and aware of his condition but seemed more concerned about how this may affect you and your children."

I said, "Yes that's just like him to be concerned about the welfare of others."

She got a serious look on her face and said, "The bad news is he is also in danger of losing his leg."

I pleaded with her, "You must tell someone to try to find his arm." Finally she told me, "There probably is no hope of finding it in good enough shape to be used as it went through the prop." I didn't want to believe any of it. This must be a dream that I would awaken from to find my husband in bed beside me.

The director of the museum, Mr. Holt, who was scheduled to be in the plane too, had canceled at the last minute. He found me and took me to Baltimore and the hospital where they had taken my husband. During the two hour drive I could only focus on the positive. I didn't dare let myself think of what might go wrong. I thought the worst must have already happened. Until now my life had been free of tragedy. Death had not been a companion. I was so young, and focused on the new life that I carried in my womb, that I hadn't given much thought to death, especially not the death of one so near and dear to me. On the ride to Baltimore, we talked about when Pete might go back to work. Mr, Holt assured me that no matter what, Pete would always have his job. The only thing I could do now was to focus on the light at the end of the tunnel instead of the tunnel I was in the middle of.

My brother, Wayne, and sister-in-law, Angel, joined me at the hospital and sat with me all night. That night seemed endless. I started to focus less on the drama and more on the moment. That was all that I had; the knowing that in the moment Pete was still alive. I could hold on to that. The doctors would come in from time to time and give us an update of his condition. With each visit there seemed less hope he would survive.

As I focused more on the moment, a peace came upon me. If I thought of the past there was the memory of terror. If I thought of the future there was the fear of losing my beloved. If I stayed in the moment I still had Pete. It was in that moment of being that I started to see through the eyes of my soul. I was no longer in the drama, no longer in my physical body. I was above the whole scene as if I was watching a movie. I no longer felt the pain in my heart or the endless tears that streaked my face. I was watching someone else in a play.

It wasn't until the early hours of the morning that the doctors finally let me see him. They had been working very hard to save him so I wasn't allowed in. Things didn't look good. The doctors came to tell me that they would have to remove his leg in an effort to save him. I had to give them permission to do this. As soon as they had finished the surgery they let me go to him.

Etched in my memory is a picture of the room they took me to and the long corridor that lead to Pete. It was too painful to be in my body so I floated just above it. I had to feel detached from the physical so that I could find the strength to see him. These may be our last moments together. There could be no falling apart now. Was it time to say goodbye – goodbye to my beloved? We had waited so long to be together and now so suddenly it felt as if he was being torn away from me, our son, and our unborn child.

As I entered the central room, the energy shifted. The air seemed almost smoke- filled. Everything had a white glow around it. I felt as if I was aboard a space ship in a surreal science fiction movie. In the center of the room there was a round elevated platform. On the platform, doctors, nurses, and technicians were intensely watching monitors and screens. The air was so full of tension you could have cut it with a knife. Spaced all around the room were various souls in the midst of transition – between the worlds. Some would choose to stay and some to leave the body. Those souls who hadn't yet decided just hung there in suspended animation or limbo. It felt as if I had stepped into another world or dimension where time stood still.

I went to Pete's side and took his hand. I had hoped he would still be conscious but he wasn't. Even though he had been through so much his face didn't show it. There were no marks or even bruises. He had a very calm and peaceful look about him. The staff had covered him in such a way that it wasn't obvious that he was missing an arm and a leg. He looked like he was just taking a nap. Oh, how I wished that were so!

The nurse standing next to me said, "He's been conscious the whole night and asking how you were. He was hoping to see you. He just lost consciousness when he was anesthetized before the surgery." She patted me on the shoulder and left us alone.

I knew my husband well and I knew he would not be happy in the body he now had. I also knew he was hanging in there for me and the children. I did the most difficult thing that I have ever done in this life time. I set him free. I looked up above the place where his body was and said out loud, "Pete, I know you well. I know it will be difficult for you to be happy in this world now. If you are hanging on for me and Jon and the baby, don't. Think about yourself. If you aren't happy we won't be. I love you but I set you free. Don't worry about us. We will be fine. Do what is best for *you.*" In my heart I knew what his choice would be. I knew I would never have the opportunity to say goodbye to his physical form. I did, however, feel complete with saying farewell to his soul.

It was at this moment, as I look back now, that I was united with the invisible worlds all around us – the other dimensions of being. I was looking through the eyes of my soul, seeing his soul.

I was taken back to the waiting room. A short time later they came in to tell me he had passed on. As the doctor very lovingly and compassionately talked to my physical body, my consciousness hovered just above the room. The words of the doctor were muffled and almost inaudible. Next to me I felt the presence of a very loving angel who made me feel safe and cared for. I heard the words, *"Do not fear for I am with thee. You never shall want for anything for you shall be taken care of. You shall be richer than you have ever dreamed. You shall never want. We watch over you. We love you."* The words were so clear, and the angel so real. It reminded me of my snowman so many years before. How could I not have faith in the angels and God?

 The doctors said I could go back in to see him. I didn't want to go. As far as I was concerned he wasn't there anymore. There seemed no sense in looking at an empty broken shell. I still had Pete in my heart and no one could take that from me. I hesitated for a few minutes and then I pulled myself together. Once again the doctor escorted me down that long corridor directly into the heart of the trauma center. I am glad that I went. It wasn't as difficult this time. I walked over to his body knowing that he wasn't there. I looked up and found him floating in midair – free to be. He was glowing just like my snowman. I raised my right arm up as high as I could and said goodbye one last time.

 As I write these words now the page is stained with tears. After seventeen years it is still difficult to take myself back to those times. When looking through the eyes of the soul, there is no time. It is as though those events are always there still happening. It had not been my intention to go off in such detail about this part of my life but how could you, the reader of these words, understand my faith in the unseen if this part of the story weren't told.

 The angels didn't waste any time showing me they meant what they said. As soon as I came back into my body another doctor came into the room. "I've been sent to take special care of you. I am a family friend of your doctor in St. Michaels. He called me and asked if I would personally be here for you." He took me to his office just upstairs, examined me, and then said, "You are doing remarkably well and so is your baby. There is no reason to believe this shock has harmed him. Would you like to listen to his heart beat?" Now I could be in the moment again. I knew everything was going to be all right. As I listened to that tiny heart beat I remembered the first time I actually saw this unborn child.

Before the accident, my husband had the opportunity to see his unborn son. I had been bleeding quite heavily and beenconfined to my bed for a month. The doctor ordered a sonogram to be sure I hadn't already lost our child. Pete took off from work and we both watched our son suck his thumb on the screen. At least that is what it looked like he might be doing. The picture was so bad it was really hard to see. The one thing that was clear was his strong heartbeat.

Just one week before the plane crash, in my third month, the bleeding suddenly stopped and never started again. I heard a voice from within telling me my son would be fine and all was being taken care of. I would not lose the baby.

The voices were sometimes very clear and sometimes just a knowing but they were with me – now a part of me. This inner knowing kept me together in those times. My faith was sustained and whenever I wanted for anything, it would somehow manifest. People who I didn't even know sent gifts of money, cards, letters, and offers of help. Thousands of dollars came in the mail. As I struggled to pay the bills, I would pray to find some way to pay them. It seemed as though when I would get down to my last dollar, there would be another check in the mailbox from someone who had known my husband and wanted to help. This went on for months then years after the accident.

At some point, a rumor was started that I was having twins, and the checks started to come again. Even though I tried to dispel the rumor people still insisted I was having twins. Years later, when in the grocery store, a woman stopped me and asked how my twins were. In small towns rumors can seem more real than the truth. I joked that the angels started the rumor and who knows, maybe they did. One thing is for sure; I felt the support of the community, and my neighbors had become my extended family.

Nothing in my life would ever be the same. It was as though a part of me, the old Joyce, left when Pete left. I had my new life, the new life within me, and our three year old son, Jonathan, to think of. I had no time to feel sorry for myself. I must stay in the moment focusing on all that must be done for our family – not the past. If I tried to look beyond what must be done today, I found myself completely overwhelmed. I was learning to live in the moment the hard way.

My husband had tried to teach me this, for he had learned the hard way as well. When I met him he had just gone into remission from cancer. Every year he went to the doctor to get his blood tested. His yearly checkup was just weeks before the accident. The doctors gave us great news – Pete had been officially cured of cancer. It had been 12 years and no reoccurence. In those years we learned how to appreciate every moment we had together.

At the beginning of our relationship, my mother asked me when I told her about Pete, "Why would you want to get involved with someone who has cancer?"

I said, "No one knows how they will die. He could just as well get hit by a truck when crossing the street. I love him *now* and want to be with him *now*." How ironic.

From the start, some part of me knew we didn't have long to be together. My logical mind thought it would be the cancer coming back that would take him away but I didn't care. I loved him so much I would be happy with whatever time we did have together, and be grateful for every moment. I was angry that just after the doctors proclaimed that he had beaten cancer and we were feeling safe, a plane took him out.

Looking back from a higher perspective I can now see the beauty of it all. What a quantum opportunity for growth. I was learning first-hand how to be present.

Chapter 2

In the seventh or eighth month of the pregnancy something happened that would make what may be called the *invisible worlds* clear and very visible.

Some friends decided that I needed to get out of the house and have some fun. I went along with them to a waterfront pub in Oxford, another small town near where we lived. I hadn't been out socially for quite some time. Conversation with my three year old son Jon, while interesting, wasn't intellectually stimulating. It was great to once again be in the company of adults.

A very tall dark man with intense black eyes came over to me and started up a conversation. I was obviously very pregnant and for that reason didn't think he could be hitting on *me*. The last thing on my mind was possible romance. He spoke with a broken accent and obviously wasn't from Oxford, Maryland. This intrigued me. Foreigners were different – exciting.

The conversation went like this..... "Where are you from? How long have you been in this country? What are you doing here.....?"

"I am from the Middle East. I have been here a few months. I am working at the hotel in town."

Then the conversation shifted to spiritual matters after I mentioned Pete and the plane crash. We became so engrossed in conversation it was as though we were on an island talking instead of in a crowded bar.

He was fascinating and intriguing but I had no physical attraction to him at all, and I wasn't aware that he had any attraction to me. We were simply sharing our own very personal beliefs and views of spirituality. It didn't seem to matter that most people would think this a very inappropriate setting for conversations dealing with creation, God, other dimensions, or life after death.

We talked for hours yet it seemed like minutes. My friends came to tell me it was time to leave but we still weren't through with the conversation. He asked, "May I have your phone number? I would like you to meet a friend of mine. I will call and we can meet tomorrow for lunch in St. Michael's."

I hesitated, surprised that he would ask for my number. This was a total stranger. I thought to myself, "If I meet him in public, during the day, and with a friend, it will be safe." I finally replied, "I guess that will be all right. Call me to make sure about the time in the morning. I have to arrange for a baby sitter for my son."

In my mind I had just met an interesting new person to share cultural views with and to learn a different way of thinking. He might help me gain greater understanding of the many questions which haunted me about the unexplained visions I had experienced. From our conversation it was clear that he had a vaster understanding of the other worlds than I did. That was my only interest in him.

One of Pete's many talents was wood working. When in college, he minored in the craft. He had designed and made much of our furniture. He made the frame for our water bed. It was one of the old style water beds. When someone got in or out, it would create a wave and roll the bed up and down.

That night as I lay quietly in this bed, after just meeting this tall dark stranger, I turned my head to the empty side of this king-sized bed. This was the time of the day that I dreaded – bedtime. I kept a large box of tissues next to the bed because I needed them every night. On the other side of the room was a crib which was also empty. The only company I had were the frequent and vigorous kicks of the baby. Resting always triggered his awakening.

I took a deep breath as I wiped away some tears when suddenly a man appeared next to me. It was the man from the pub. He still had on the same clothes. He had his arms crossed over his chest and he was lying straight out on top of the covers where my husband had slept. He appeared out of nowhere – so suddenly – not a ripple was felt in the water bed. He was very solid. This wasn't like the snowman that I could almost see through. This man had physically manifested in this dimension. He turned his head and grinned at me. Well! To say I was shocked was an understatement. Almost immediately I quite forcefully said, "How dare you intrude in my bed? Get out *now*!" He disappeared instantly.

It's always been my style to fall apart after the fact. I'm great in the moment but when looking back at what might have occurred I fall apart. The past can bring up my fear and doubt. Questions would arise. What happened? Did I do the right thing? Did I bring this on? What should I have done differently? And then the obvious; how can I keep it from happening again?

The next morning my fears were rampant. I felt totally violated and intruded upon. How dare this man take such liberties – and with a pregnant woman. My imagination played out all sorts of intriguing possibilities about him and what he wanted of me. I sat by the phone almost afraid it would ring. Maybe he wouldn't call. Maybe he would lose the number and I would never hear from him again. Maybe after sending him away so forcefully from my bed, he would be too ashamed to contact me again. He had really scared me. For the first time in my life, the unknown scared me. The unknown that I had longed to understand had shocked the hell out of me.

The phone rang. I gathered my courage and got back into the moment where I was just picking up the phone in my kitchen. Something I did every day. "Hello."

"May I speak to Joyce?"

"This is Joyce."

"Joyce this is the man you met last night. I'm at a restaurant in St. Michaels with my friend. Can you join us for lunch?"

How dare he have the nerve to call me after last night. He acted like nothing had happened. My mind raced as I thought up an excuse to get out of the meeting. Then I got angry. He wasn't worth wasting a lie for, so I blurted out, "How dare you call me? Wasn't what you did last night enough?"

"What did I do?"

"You know very well what you did. I never want to see you again so don't call." I hung the phone up and that was that.

In that moment I wasn't capable of seeing through the eyes of my soul. The only view I had was fear based. My fear kept me from ever finding out if this man was actually aware of anything that had happened. Maybe he didn't even know that he had bi-located and manifested next to me in bed. Today I would have still been angry at the intrusion but not out of fear. Now I would handle the situation far differently; however all was perfect as it occurred. Judgment of self is not necessary. No wouda, shoulda, coulda's now – only opportunities for growth in the moment.

Chapter 3

Michael Gedeon came into the world on May 7th, 1984. The crib next to my bed would no longer be empty. I was two weeks late and the labor went on for two days. Mikie hadn't wanted to come into this world. He hung on to my ribs, and after two days of labor, had to be cut out. We stayed in the hospital for a week – I enjoyed the rest. When I went home I would have to do it alone and I wasn't looking forward to that.

The angels were at work again and I was given a private nurse. We had many common interests and later became good friends. She would join our meditation group. I also had a private room and was able to have my new baby in the room with me. Most mothers were sent home in a few days but I was given a lot more time than most new mothers.

God had blessed me with a healthy and peaceful soul who slept through the night from the start. When visiting the doctor's office I asked if something might be wrong with him because he seemed to sleep all the time.

The doctor just laughed and said, "That's normal."

Our first born was just the opposite of Mikie. Jon never slept or took naps. In time, the boys would become opposite in almost every way.

The three of us along with my brother-in-law, Ed, settled into a new life together. About a year before my husband's accident, I had suggested to Pete (though I didn't understand why) that we invite his brother to come and live with us. This was before we knew about a baby coming. Pete's brother was just out of high school; the economy was slow, and he was looking for a job.

Ed lived with my husband's family in Ohio. It was a small town and there weren't many jobs for him to find there. Pete was able to get a job for Ed in Easton. Because of the great difference in their age, they hadn't had the opportunity to get to know each other because Pete left home for college soon after his mother gave birth to Ed.

We had a spare room and I imagined that this would only be a short term arrangement – six months at most. Then I found out that I was pregnant. Money became an issue. I could no longer work because I was spotting. The doctor instructed me to stay in bed as much as possible. Pete would not ask his brother for money or to find another place to live. We argued over this frequently.

A friend called me and said, "You must be a saint, to keep your husband's brother for so long. I don't think I would have been that generous."

I said, "Well, he needs us now. Who knows maybe someday we will need him."

At the time I had no idea how true those words were. There had just been a knowing that we should have him with us. It didn't make any logical sense. Just one week after that conversation Pete was in the plane crash. Eddie was there helping me, and most of all, helping Jon, who had grown close to him. My brother-in-law was like an angel who had been sent to help us.

Shortly after my husband's passing my father, Philip had a heart attack. He and my mother, Mary, lived in Baltimore. From St. Michaels, Baltimore is almost a two hour drive. My mother had been born and lived her whole life in the suburbs of the city. Hating the city, I left as soon as it was possible. When Pete had gotten his job in St. Michaels, I was happy because I had roots there. My father had been born and raised in that sleepy waterfront town.

For as long as I could remember, our family would make the drive to visit my grandparents in Easton which was just outside St. Michaels. As I drove by myself to go to see my ill father, I thought about those wonderful trips we took as a family. In my mind I could hear my brother and me arguing in the back seat and my mother telling us, "Be quiet, so your father can drive safely." As I drove across the long Chesapeake Bay Bridge, I recalled the days before the bridge had been built – when we took the ferry to get to the other side. Now there were two bridges. As I drove to the hospital to be with my father, I slipped out of the moment and memories flooded my awareness.

When I focused on the past, my fears returned and so did my issues of abandonment. This heart attack caught us all by surprise. My father had, on the surface, seemed very healthy. Memories of other tragic surprises that involved men who had been close to my heart surfaced. Of course there had been my husband but there was another memory that had been even earlier.

Joey was my first boyfriend. He lived just two doors down and his mother was godmother to my brother Wayne. We met when we were just babies. He was one year younger than I. We usually got along just great. He was an only child and got into a lot of mischief.

Joey had a bad habit of biting me every once in a while for no apparent reason. Other than that we got along just fine. It was fun having him around because he was always in some kind of trouble and that was exciting.

The day of my baby brother's christening, we would have been about four and five. The whole family was gathered along with Joey's parents. His mom, who I called Aunt Claire, was the neighbor who heard my screams when I was visited by the snowman. I remember this day very clearly because it was the day we got into the worst trouble ever.

My mother is Italian and one of twelve children. Her large, mostly Catholic family took this day quite seriously. Everyone was wearing their Sunday best clothes. My father, who was English only had three brothers. Not too many of his relations came, but then most of them lived in St. Michaels. Most were farmers and never left their farms. There was a lot of food and wall-to-wall people in our little two bedroom bungalow.

I really wasn't sure what all the fuss was about. I thought, "All my new brother does is cry and get in my way. They even put him in my bedroom. Why is everyone looking at him?"

Joey came with a squirt gun and proceeded to chase me all over the house with it. I didn't want to get my new dress wet so I ran away from him. He was relentless and he cornered me in the bathroom. I locked myself in. There was no way out and I knew he was not going to give up. I didn't want to spend the whole day in this horrible little room.

My creative mind devised a plan; I would retaliate. The only reason he had me cornered was because I didn't have my own squirt gun to shoot him back. I looked around the bathroom for something I could use to get even with him. Just under the sink I struck gold. I found the perfect thing to use and I quickly filled it with water. I was now grateful for being in the bathroom. If I had been stuck in another room, my plan would not have worked.

Joey was still outside the door trying to open it and banging on it. I unlocked it, stepped back, and said, "Ok. You win. I quit. You can come in now." He opened the door and held up his freshly loaded gun but I let him have it before he could squeeze the trigger. With one squeeze I drenched him from head to toe and sent him screaming in the other direction. I quickly reloaded and chased him all through the house and in the process managing to dampen the whole christening party. Everyone sat in shock and amazement at the sight of me chasing Joey with my mother's douche bulb!

My mother must have been totally humiliated and embarrassed. I, on the other hand, was now the center of everyone's attention.

This was the kind of love-hate relationship Joey and I had. I tell you about it now because Joey was the first man in my life to die and leave me.

Our family moved to the other side of town when I was in the third grade. Joey had just made his first Holy Communion and we went to visit him at his house. I was looking forward to getting into some trouble with him. Things had been pretty boring in my new neighborhood. No one bit me or chased me and part of me missed the excitement.

We went up to the attic to play and immediately I noticed something different about Joey. He had a white glow all around him and he sat peacefully on the chair. The conversation went like this, "Do you feel all right? You look different. Let's go do something bad."

He didn't say much, just this, "I'm different now. I have Jesus with me. I don't have to do those things anymore." All he wanted to do was sit and look at me. He didn't even try to bite me.

As we drove home, from the back seat of the car I said, "Mom. If you tell someone who's been bad to you that when they die they will go to hell and the devil, will that really happen because you said it?"

"No honey. That's silly. You aren't God. And anyway, there probably isn't a hell or a devil. Why are you talking like that?"

"Oh, once when Joey bit me so hard that he drew blood, I told him he would go to be with the Devil in Hell. Now that he's going to die, and he isn't biting me anymore, I don't want him to go there because of me."

"Why would you think Joey is dying?" my mom asked.

I said, "He has a white glow all around him and he is just like Jesus – too good to be here. I just know he is going to die."

"It's not nice to talk that way. Never say to anyone you think people are going to die or that you see things. And never talk about this again to anyone. Joey isn't sick. There is nothing wrong with him and he is not going to die."

I sat back in my seat and did what I was told. What Mom said must be true. I had learned from the past that no one believed what I saw anyway so why argue with her now?

About one week later, I found my mother on the phone and in tears as I came in the house from school. She stopped her conversation and said to me, "I have some terrible news...."

I said very calmly before she could finish, "I know. Joey died."

She looked as if she might drop the phone. "How did you know?"

"Don't you remember? I told you he was going to die."

It didn't bother me that he had died. Oh, I would miss him and the old days of mischief but I knew that Joey was where he wanted to be – with the angels and Jesus. I also knew because my mother told me that he was not in hell because of me. That was a great relief.

They buried him on the hill behind my house in the Catholic cemetery. His mother put a statue of an angel on his grave site and from my bedroom window, showed me how I could see his grave even though it was pretty far away. I never could understand why she thought that would make me feel better. It was as though she thought he was in the ground. I knew he would never be there. He was having fun playing with the angels.

Aunt Claire came to visit us often. She went to his graveside almost every Sunday and for sure on holidays. It was easy to make out his plot from my window because it always had the most color around it. Joey had been Aunt Claire's only child and she never really got over his loss. She came up to my room one Sunday and took me to the window to make sure I could still remember where she thought he was. "There's something I have always wanted to tell you Joycie. Joey loved you very much. You were his favorite."

"Then why did he bite me all the time Aunt Claire?"

She had a tear in her eye and she said, "I suppose he just got a little carried away with his love. That was just his way of showing affection. When he was very young we would affectionately nibble his fingers and toes. He must have interpreted the love bites as a way of showing love. The more intense the love the stronger the bite would have to be. He clearly loved you best because he bit you the hardest."

Finally I understood and could forgive him.

Joey taught me early in life that things weren't always what they appeared to be on the surface. He taught me that everyone has a different way of loving and expressing that love. Many times love is misinterpreted – misunderstood. What was really important wasn't the actual expression but the love itself.

As I stopped thinking of the past and Joey, my attention turned again to the moment and my daddy in the hospital. Was there some pattern in my life that had to do with being abandoned by the men who I loved and who loved me?

My father, whose name was Philip, survived this heart attack and seven years later he joined Joey on the other side. Pete's passing had been sudden and unexpected. My father's soul had chosen just the opposite. His funeral was a celebration. It was clear to everyone that my father longed for release from his physical body. It had become a prison that he felt he had no control over. The grief I experienced was for our loss not his. For him there was freedom.

My father and I were blessed with plenty of time to talk and get closer on the numerous occasions that he was hospitalized. Each visit was a gift – a painful one – but a gift I didn't have with my husband.

On one of those visits we talked about things that surprised even me. For the first time in my life, this usually quiet man was sharing his innermost feelings. His condition had deteriorated, and the doctors told him that he must have his gall bladder removed. The pain he was experiencing was weakening his heart. There was one catch; they didn't think they could do the surgery. It had been only a few months since he had a quadruple by-pass and anesthesia was out of the question.

The hospital was one of the best, Johns Hopkins. My dad convinced his physician to do the surgery without anesthesia. The doctor was from India and was familiar with the out-of-body meditation that my dad said he was able to do. So the doctor only used Novocain to do the surgery.

I was sitting next to my father shortly after the operation. It had been a complete success and he was feeling much better – no pain at last. A group of interns came into the room to talk with him... "Mr. Swann we have a question for you. Are you sure you didn't feel anything during the surgery?"

My father looked up at them and grinned, then said, "No, I felt nothing – I wasn't there." They just shook their heads and walked out of the room.

Then we had a conversation that went something like this...
"Dad, how did you do it?"

"Remember when you were just a little girl and your mother and I had gotten a lot of books from the library about ESP and mind reading?"

"Yes, I remember you and mom sitting in separate rooms guessing what the other one had written on a piece of paper."

"That wasn't all that I did. I read a book on out-of-body experiences and decided to experiment. One night as I lay in my bed, I projected myself up above the house. It scared the shit out of me. I was afraid that I wouldn't be able to get back and I never tried it again. We took the books back to the library and we never discussed it again. When the doctor told me my options – which were none – I knew I could do it again. I didn't have that fear of leaving my body anymore."

My father gave me a great gift. He had conquered his fear of the unknown – the unexplainable – and given that freedom to me.

Now, I was able to share that part of me that I thought no one could ever understand and until then even I didn't understand. We talked about the snowman and much more. He believed me now. We had a special bond. He helped me to understand why it looked like the ceiling would move at night and the stars would come into the room. Until that day, I didn't realize that I had been out of my body.

On one of our visits, I gave him a copy of a small booklet that I had written. This was the first channeled material that I had put together. I was able to explain how easily the words would flow and I would just write them down, not consciously knowing where any given thought might take me. I told him I no longer wanted to make things like sculpture, but saw writing as my new way of expressing creativity.

When I returned the next day to the hospital, he thanked me for the book and said, "I was too weak to read it by myself but the man from across the hall read it to me. I loved it and so did he. I am happy for you. I'm glad you found this gift and want to share it with others."

Chapter 4

Early this morning I awakened from a dream or was it reality? I'm in the middle of a dream production – widescreen, Technicolor, and Cinema Scope. Then I come back into my body and open my eyes only to realize it was just another story. One might call this the dream tapestry. This realization reminded me of yet another story. They are never-ending. I am in the habit of writing down my dreams as soon as I awaken so they can be remembered and then learned from.

This morning, the dream seemed to be happening while I was awake. I was reliving a story that happened years before. It seemed so real – like it was still happening. This was not something I wanted to remember and certainly not relive or write about. It is about a woman who doesn't exist anymore and one I'd just as soon forget. However, I was that woman and she helped to create who I now am.

Why had I brought back this terrible memory? As I tried to go back to sleep, my mind went to the night before. The television was on and I felt compelled to watch a show about elderly men being preyed upon by young women. The show reminded me of Marty. All I had to do was change the sexes of the characters and their ages to find the same story, but thankfully not the same ending. Determined *not* to tell the story to you, the reader, I got up and went

to feed the chickens, and stoke the wood stove that heats our house –
anything would be better than writing about Marty. Then while
seated on the throne, ideas started flooding me as they many times
did.

It may seem odd that I would get material – guidance – in the
bathroom while sitting on, of all things, the toilet. I'm not sure why
but it is true. This was the room where I got the inspiration to use
that now infamous weapon of water destruction that will go down in
our families' history as memorable. There must be something about
opening, releasing, and letting go while seated on the throne of
inspiration. Maybe it's the energy of the water just below. For
whatever reason, years ago I realized that when emerging from this
facility, the questions that I had when entering were answered when
I departed. Often during group sessions, or workshops that I was
leading, I would excuse myself if someone asked a question that
there seemed no answer for, and go to the throne for advice. I've
never been disappointed.

Since I have so much respect for this high authority, there
was now no denying my ultimate fate. I must bare all. (slight pun)

This part of the tapestry was created three years after my
husband journeyed to the other dimensions. Joey was gone; my
husband was gone; my father was gone; and now Ed, my brother-in-
law, was getting married and leaving. There would just be the three
of us.

This memory was written as if it were fiction and the main
character someone other than myself. This is appropriate since she
is no longer who I am.

Joyce hadn't dated anyone since she lost her husband three years ago in a plane crash. She was feeling the stresses of her new role as both mother and father; caring for her two children, Jon, six, and Mike, two, and earning whatever she could when she wasn't taking care of them. She had been teaching water aerobics and exercising at the fitness center whenever possible. She was slender and not too hard on the eyes.

It had been many years since she had been single. There seemed to be something missing in her life – an emptiness that needed to be filled once more. So feeling good about her body again, after what seemed like an eternal pregnancy, Joyce was ready to meet Marty.

He appeared on the scene, a tall, impressive looking man. Not who some would call handsome but striking in appearance with a magnetic personality. He was a person everyone instantly liked. Joyce was introduced to him at a party given by one of her friends who may have been playing matchmaker. As they talked she discovered this man had much in common with her late husband Pete. Marty told her whatever she needed to hear and she is hooked. He wasted no time wining and dining her, bringing her expensive presents, and making himself indispensable to her and the two boys.

In this whirlwind romance she is beginning to feel like Cinderella. Her prince Marty told her he is very wealthy and his only desire is to shower her with love and support. He told her he can give her all the things missing in her lonely life. It seems almost too good to be true, perfect in every way – any woman's dream of husband and father to the children. He cooks, cleans, and attends to her every need and desire. The joy that had been so missed was back in her life. While the dream seemed real the nightmare was just around the corner, waiting to unfold.

In what appeared a short time, but seemed an eternity, Marty proposed marriage. How could she say no to this package! He seemed to answer her every prayer and even the boys loved him. Marty had a way of getting the children to willingly do whatever he asked. It was easy for her to say *yes*, when he proposed that they marry and become one big happy family.

He told her his father was a retired diplomat living in Colorado on an enormous cattle ranch. He was an only son and his parents wanted to give them a wedding present – a house! They went shopping for the perfect house and found it just outside St. Michaels, at a cost of only $170,000. This seemed like nothing to Marty but it really impressed Joyce. Marty had moved into her house and one day when he returned from his job, he presented her with the contract on the house for her to sign. This would make it legal. The paper had the letter head from the realtors that had shown the house to them. She could scarcely believe it but there was the contract. The closing date was set for three months later.

Because of the imminent marriage and move, Marty started to go through the attic, packing up and even selling some of her things in preparation. It was amazing how many of the things she had that Marty said he already owned. All of his things, were of course, in Colorado and because as he said he had more money, the quality of his things was always better. The reasoning was to get rid of the excess so there would be less to do later during the move. He was glad to help her do the extra work. How thoughtful.

Although things were moving fast, they weren't moving fast enough for Marty. Only three months had gone by and Joyce was starting to get an uneasy feeling about his great hurry to marry and adopt the boys. She reasoned that even though she had seen the mortgage papers on the new house, she hadn't met Marty's parents who had given it to them. She was beginning to have little doubts and felt that this all seemed too good to be true.

She heard about a gifted psychic who was in town and who had given an incredible reading to one of her friends. Joyce had never been to a psychic but she needed advice from someone who had never met Marty.

Marty wasn't pleased about the idea. In fact he didn't want her to have any outside input. In his opinion he was all she needed. Her friends were starting to question why she had little communication with them and one friend even questioned his motives.

Joyce wanted to keep him perfect so she ignored her friends and listened to him. Marty pointed out that they were happier when her friends weren't interfering. "They're just jealous because they have no husbands and little money," he would say. Still she felt compelled to see the psychic whether he liked it or not. Joyce had an independent spirit and didn't like to be told what to do.

Upon entering the room where the mystic sat she noticed that the atmosphere felt electric. It brought back the memory of the room in the hospital where she had visited her husband and said her last good-byes. There was an air of anxious anticipation within her.

A very pleasant yet serious middle-aged woman sat on a studio bed. She was African and spoke with a heavy accent. She called Joyce over to sit next to her on the bed. They held hands and the woman looked all around and behind Joyce. "What protection you have. Many guides and angels. You have nothing to fear. You are well protected." Joyce thought to herself, "Why do I need so much protection?" The woman went on, "You are very attracted to a man who has many women in his life. He lies a lot and sometimes even forgets what the real truth is. You will catch him in his lies by asking the same things to him and noticing the slight differences in his answers. Eventually he will expose himself through his lies because of your persistent questions."

A part of Joyce was ready to give up the relationship and yet another part wasn't. She asked, "Should I end this relationship since he is a liar?"

"No. Proceed as if everything is the same and know that you are well protected. He is part of your purpose. Just remember to always question him until you catch him. Whatever you do, don't let him take you to his cattle ranch. Stay in St. Michaels. Your husband is trying to communicate with you. That is why doors have been slamming and things have been falling off shelves. He is trying to get your attention. He is not jealous of your new love. Listen to him."

Joyce left the psychic visibly shaken. So much of what she said was true. How did this stranger know that Marty had a cattle ranch in Colorado? How did she know about all the weird things happening in the house since Marty first came? It was true. Doors would open and close on their own. Books would fall off shelves and objects would disappear more often than usual. She had suspected that it was her husband and thought he was jealous of her new love. She even told Marty on occasion, "That's just my husband. He doesn't want you here."

When she went home, Marty asked her about the psychic. She decided to tell him just a part of what the woman had said and made light of the whole experience. Her reasoning was to see what his reaction would be and pretend that she thought it was absurd. For the first time he was speechless as she told him this woman knew he had a cattle ranch.

Was this warning real? Would Cinderella turn into Little Red Riding Hood? Was Prince Charming really the Big Bad Wolf in disguise? She wondered if her new house would turn into a pumpkin.

As a result of the reading, she decided to proceed more cautiously with the relationship. She would only marry Marty after she met his parents, and insisted on a prenuptial agreement. Marty called Colorado and arranged for his parents to meet them in Washington, D.C. It seemed his father had some diplomatic business in the area to attend to and they could meet at nearby Williamsburg and have a brief vacation with the boys too. His mother was bringing her engagement ring – a family heirloom.

Before they left for this holiday, she wanted to get in touch with her lawyer to start work on the prenuptial agreement. She told Marty she was only doing this to protect the interests of her sons' inheritance. Marty didn't understand why this was needed. After all he had all the money in the family, or would have, as the sole heir of his parents' considerable estate and the 10,000 acre cattle ranch in Colorado.

Joyce was playing it safe. She ignored what he said and called her lawyer. When she told Marty she was waiting for a call back, he told her, "Lawyers never call back. You'll probably have to wait a long time to hear from them." A few days later they all went to Williamsburg, Virginia. He was right; the lawyers hadn't called back. In fact, the phone never seemed to ring anymore. She would call again when they got back.

The motel was very nice. Marty played in the pool with the boys and everyone had fun. They were like a family on vacation. He was a bit embarrassed because his funds were very low. He wondered if he could have a loan just until he saw his father. So the trip was now paid for by Joyce.

More and more she was questioning Marty as the psychic had instructed her. She was feeling almost as if she had woken up in a dream, questioning what was real and what wasn't, and trying to make sense of it all. She played along as if she had no doubts. No decisions about a wedding would be made until she met his parents.

On the morning his parents were to meet them in Williamsburg a call woke them up very early. Marty answered the phone. All Joyce heard was his side of the conversation. From that she gathered it was the state police. His parents had been in a serious car accident just outside Washington. They were rushed to Bethesda Naval Hospital where they were listed in serious condition. Marty said no visitors were allowed because it was a restricted area on the naval base and they were in intensive care. The Big Bad Wolf was crying crocodile tears and Sleeping Beauty was waking up from a long sleep.

Her husband, Pete, had retired from the Navy. She knew that the hospital was not restricted. She also knew there were no such rules about visitation. What Marty had told her was a lie; the first of many she would catch him in. Anyone could visit a naval hospital – especially the families of patients. She confronted him, and he then said, "What I meant to say is that I am the only one they will let in and anyway I don't want to see them in that condition. I hate hospitals."

They went back to St. Michaels to await news of his parents there. Joyce called her lawyer when they returned and they told her they had been calling her for days but the phone rang and no one answered. She discovered that something was wrong with the phone and it didn't ring even though calls could still be made. The telephone man was called to fix it. The repair man informed them that an outside wire had been cut. Marty blamed the boys for it saying, "I saw them playing around the box where the line was cut." It was fixed but not for long.

A part of Joyce was in complete denial, desperately not wanting to believe the worst; that Marty was a total lie. She was afraid of waking up from a fairy tale dream to find herself in a dreadful nightmare. Not able to choose between the two possibilities, she began to live them both simultaneously. This is what would save her. While pretending to believe everything Marty told her, another Joyce was coalescing. Floating just above her was another being who didn't believe anything and questioned everything. This part of herself was waking up and putting the pieces together – seeing through the eyes of the soul.

It all seemed too fantastic to be true. What was she to believe? Both views seemed unreal. There was the Cinderella story she wanted to believe. And then there was the story of Little Red Riding Hood – that tempting victim and the cunning Big Bad Wolf – that she still had to prove existed and didn't want to be true. She wished she could awaken and discover it had all been a bad dream, but there seemed no way out. She remembered being told that she was protected and this comforted her as the curtain rose on the third and final act of this grand play.

Marty was nervous and jumpy. He said it was because he was so worried about his parents but maybe it was really because he was afraid of getting caught in his lies. The pressure was building. He was on the phone in constant communication with the naval hospital. There were several calls made to Colorado to tell friends and family about the accident. Things were looking bad. Joyce encouraged him to go back to the Washington area to be close to the hospital in case his parents took a turn for the worse. He agreed this would be best but wouldn't go without her. The phone was not ringing again so Marty called the phone company for the second time to get it fixed. Joyce took the boys across the street to stay with a neighbor while they were gone. There seemed less stress without them and less to take care of.

Still not wanting to believe the worst, Cinderella left for D.C. with the grieving Prince Charming. When the clock struck midnight would her fairy prince turn into the Big Bad Wolf? She was so caught up in the drama there seemed no choice but to follow Marty to Bethesda and try to see his parents one more time. Did they exist or were they just part of an elaborate scam, ingeniously created by a professional con artist?

This time he took her to a remote run down motel. She paid for everything again. Marty had quit his job. He said he was stressed out over the accident and would be dependent on her until he inherited his fortune. He called the hospital from the hotel room but still no visitors were allowed. Calls would come in the morning giving reports of their condition. He would always jump to answer the phone first.

The part of Joyce that had awakened realized he must have been answering wake up calls from the desk clerk all along. He would go to check in at the hotel, ask for a wakeup call in the morning, and then pretend it was the state police or the hospital. She was almost positive now that the next call would be telling him his parents had died. Then there would be no one for her to meet before the wedding. How convenient.

Sure enough, the wakeup call came and Marty pretended to be talking to someone at the hospital, while all along he was talking to a very confused desk clerk who called to tell him it was time to get up. Now his next move was predictable.

As she woke up to the truth and her worst fears became a reality, it was even more important to keep up the pretense that she believed him. She realized she was quite vulnerable with him and away from her home. The psychic had said not to let him take her away from St. Michaels.

Marty must have sensed that she hadn't totally believed his story and he got even more nervous. He went to the window and saw two police cars in the parking lot of the motel. He seemed to panic and as soon as the police left he suggested they go to a park he had seen on the way to the motel. He needed to be in nature to mourn the loss of his parents. He insisted she come with him and then they could get breakfast.

As they pulled up to an intersection, a truck cut their car off. It didn't seem like much of an incident to her but Marty flew into a rage. He revealed a side of himself that he had kept well hidden. His mask was finally off, and the Big Bad Wolf was staring at Little Red Riding Hood. She knew she was in danger yet she had to keep calm. It was as though she was out of her body and totally detached from the drama. She noticed a knife had appeared on the dash of the car. It had been her husband's rigging knife from his sailing days. She now knew she was going off with a crazed man who had a visible weapon, to a deserted state park very early in the morning. She was terrified but couldn't show it.

What the wolf didn't know was that on this day, a once-a-year event was scheduled to take place in the park. When they got there the grounds were already full of people preparing for this special event – an outdoor play and festival. Not at all what he had expected.

She seized the moment and put on the performance of her life, totally convincing him of her faith in him, and consoling him in his hour of need. She promised to stand by him, marry him, and always be there for him. She talked of how she had felt when she lost her husband. She pretended to understand how he must be feeling. She was convincing him that she was dumb enough to believe everything he had told her. Joyce suggested they head back home and stop in Annapolis, as walking by the harbor and being near the water might take his mind off his grief. They could get lunch and then go home to tell the boys about the death of his parents.

By planning for the future, she hoped to turn his attention around. She reasoned that if he thought he could get still more from her, maybe he would decide to take her back to St. Michaels where he stood to gain.

They talked about the plans for the funeral. Marty explained to her that there would be no open caskets. The accident had been too awful. He was the only living family so only a small group of close friends would attend the funeral on the ranch in Colorado. Their bodies would be waiting for them when they arrived and his parents would be buried on the ranch.

The act that she put on must have convinced him. She had out-conned a con. Her ability to let go of fear and to act out the play was what saved her. It was in Annapolis that she totally fooled him. He was able to relax a bit. Marty's downfall proved to be his ego that wanted to believe he was a clever con.

As soon as they pulled up in front of the garage in St. Michaels he offered to unload the car. She took her overnight case with her. Marty had convinced her to pack her best jewelry to impress his parents. She had put all her valuables in the overnight bag to keep them safe. While he was unloading the car she would phone the real estate agent that had arranged the sale of the house they were supposed to own. Knowing what she now did and being on her turf, she had to get something concrete to confront him with. If everything about him was a lie the agent would confirm it.

The phone hadn't rung but when she picked it up, her neighbor was on the other end. She then realized Marty must have cut the phone lines so that the ringer didn't work. The boys never messed with the lines; it had been Marty who cut them twice. Betty, who lived in the next house, told her that Joyce's mother was worried. Apparently, suspecting something was wrong, her brother had called the hospital to ask about the condition of Marty's parents only to be told there was no one there by that name. They had never been admitted. Joyce told Betty to call her mother back and tell her not to worry. She was already aware of the situation and would call her mother later.

Marty came in while she was talking and wanted to know why she was on the phone. Thinking quickly she told him she had picked up the phone to call the sitter and was told her father had a heart attack and it was important to call her mother. Joyce knew that Marty was aware of her father's two recent heart attacks so this seemed a believable story.

When he went back out to finish unloading the car Joyce called the real estate agent to get the last nail for Marty's coffin. Before she could even ask the agent about the sale of the house, he asked her if she knew who was spreading the rumor that the house he had shown them had been sold. He was having difficulty getting other agents to show the house because someone had spread this rumor. Now there was no doubt. There was no way Marty could explain this!

It was time to confront the Big Bad Wolf. Maybe her courage came because she still didn't believe it could be happening to her, or maybe it was because she had faith she was being guided and protected. In any event, when Marty came back into the house this time she asked him to sit down. There was something they must talk about. Seating him near the door she calmly told him that she had spoken to her mother. She confronted him with what her brother had said about his parents not being in the hospital. He immediately burst into tears. How could she not believe him? He put on his best performance, trying to convince her to get the boys and go back to D.C. with him. He would show her his dead parents and they could all go off to Colorado. There must have been a mistake at the hospital with the names.

Of course I didn't go with him. I had awakened from the nightmare and there in front of me was this pathetic and very sick man reduced to tears. He just wanted to prove to me that he wasn't a total lie. I chose not to tell him about my call to the real estate agent. I thought it was safer just to let him go. He had been planning to get his hair cut for the funeral so I suggested he go to town now to get it done. When he returned, he could prove himself to me.

I knew when he left I would never see him again. He ran like a scared rabbit. I had found great strength in my faith and it saw me through. What I didn't know was while he was in the garage getting his car out, he had packed it up with all of the things that we had planned to sell in the yard sale. He could sell my things to get seed money for his next victim.

I called the police immediately but they didn't pursue him. They said it was too late in the day to get a warrant for his arrest. They said it was a domestic quarrel and they acted like they didn't believe my story. It must have sounded too outrageous. Until I had a warrant they wouldn't go after him and I wasn't allowed to swear it out until the next morning. By then he was well out of the state.

My neighbor, Betty, who had been suspicious of him all along, peeked in the garage while we were gone and got the license number off his car. Marty had covered the windows of the garage with sheets. He said it was to keep out any burglars. Betty was able to see through a crack in the sheets. There was only one road out of town which went on for fifteen miles. The first thing I told the police when I called was that I had his license number. They could have caught him if they had tried but obviously they thought I was some disgruntled housewife who had a fight with her boyfriend and they were reluctant to get involved. I also gave them the phone number in Colorado that he had been calling. He must have had some connection there because the calls were on my phone bill.

The authorities were soon sorry that they hadn't listened to me. The next morning when I went in to swear out the warrant, they told me there was already a warrant out for his arrest. It was filed by the restaurant owner where he had been a cook. Apparently a lot of money, food, and flower arrangements were missing and so was Marty. We had eaten the lobster, and the flowers were in my front hall – a present from Prince Charming. It seemed everything he had given me was stolen. When they ran a check on the license plate, they found that the car was stolen. The owner, a young woman from Virginia Beach, was missing and to my knowledge, was never found. She hadn't been as well protected as I was.

A further check revealed that Marty had many aliases – even his name was a lie. He was being sought by the police in several states. His last victim had been a woman in Ocean City, Maryland. He was living with her and when she came home from work one day, she found an empty apartment. That was where he got the seed money to come after me. He had mentioned that he had a friend in the Navy who had access to the computers. That must have been how he knew all about me and what my husband was like. This knowledge would allow him to try to take Pete's place.

Had this been an elaborate plan that started in Norfolk at the naval base? Is that where he found out about me, the recent widow of a retired Navy man, and perfect victim for his latest scam? I probably will never know exactly how things started. The police could tell me very little because they said there were laws to protect the criminal. They did tell me that he had been an inmate in the New York state prison system, but they wouldn't tell me what he had been convicted of.

My fears didn't take hold completely until he was gone. Then I felt raped, totally violated, humiliated and victimized, not just by him but also by the police who were supposed to protect me and seemed more concerned about his welfare than mine. I immediately went to see my doctor. He did some tests just to put my mind at rest that I hadn't caught anything from Marty – AIDS was a fear now.

Then there was the thought of having to face everyone in that small town with the real truth.

The authorities told me not to stay in my own house in case Marty came back. They said he was dangerous. I had to change all the locks on the doors since he had keys. I was afraid to be in my own home. Again, I became two people – one knowing he would never return – the other fearing that he just might. So I went on a trip to visit my good friend Jean who was living in Georgia. I was too much of a wreck to take care of the boys so the Gibsons, who lived across the street, came to my rescue once more and watched them for a week. A train ride sounded like a good idea, so I got a ticket for Amtrak and set off for Georgia while attempting to leave my fears behind me.

I wrote the entire way to Georgia, recounting every detail of what had happened. If they did catch Marty, or whatever his name really was, I would be ready to testify against him, and see justice done. When I got to my friend's house, we made an audio cassette as I told her the entire fantastic story.

This proved to be only a part of the healing process. Marty was, to my knowledge, never caught and several years later the case was finally closed. As I was riding and writing on the train, I remember thinking to myself, "This would make a good movie; and I actually lived it." It was still difficult for me to believe that any of it ever happened.

When I came home, still hurting from my first unsuccessful romance and great love, a close friend named Kathy gave me the best medicine. She wasn't judging me; it wasn't wrong to love, but what I had loved was a total lie so it never really existed. She said, "How can you love a lie?"

A short time later I visited the psychic again. She told me I had been the only woman who had ever caught him and had the courage to confront him with the truth.

Now I can honestly thank Marty for helping me wake up to who I really am. I thank him for showing me that I was playing the role of the victim, a role I didn't realize I had been playing most of my life. I didn't know how to love myself. I was looking for love outside of myself.

Who am I? Just an ordinary person, a soul, with the simple desire to love and be loved unconditionally.

With all Marty had done I still didn't hate him. When I look through the eyes of the soul, I see a scared little boy who lived in an illusionary world he created because he didn't love himself. If he didn't love himself, how could anyone else possibly love him? So he made up what he thought people wanted him to be so he could feel loved. The sad part was he was caught in what he had created. He must have felt helpless to get out having lived for so long in the illusion. He had become the lie.

I had also been in fear and at that time unable to love myself. So in many ways we were alike. Thank you Marty for waking me up so I no longer have to play the role of the victim.

The state trooper who had handled the case kept coming back to see me, and every time, he asked the same question, "Have you had any contact with Marty?" It was now two years later. My friend Jean had divorced and had moved in to help with the mortgage. A picture of her and her two boys was on the top of the Hammond organ, just inside the front door.

The trooper was at the door again and I was annoyed. Every time he came in uniform and in the police car, it reminded me of the day the harbor patrol came to tell me about Pete.

I didn't like his constant probing questions. It just reminded me of that terrible nightmare. Again he asked, "Has Marty made contact with you?"

I didn't let him in the house this time. I just asked, "Why do you keep coming back over and over asking the same questions? He is never coming back. He is long gone from here."

He grinned at me and said, "Would you go out to dinner with me?"

I felt raped all over again. I thought of all the intimate questions he had asked that he may not have needed to. Questions that just told him more personal information about me and my relationship with Marty. What a creep. He had told me he was married and had six children. There was no way I would go out with this opportunist. I very simply and clearly said, "NO."

He looked at me in complete amazement and said, "What do you mean, you won't go out with me. Why not?"

To say he had a big ego was an understatement. Again I said, "NO."

"But why not?" As I answered for the last time, "Because I just don't want to."

He looked at the picture on the organ of my best friend Jean and her two sons. He grinned and said, "Oh....."

This cocky, arrogant public servant couldn't believe that I didn't find him attractive – so *I* must be gay. I said nothing just closed the door on him.

A few years later when I was visiting the local unemployment office, he came in. He was now driving a different vehicle and wearing a different uniform. He was now a delivery man for UPS.

I overheard part of the conversation. He was checking on a possible job. His wife had left him with six children and he needed another part-time job. I asked the women behind the counter if she knew anything about him and she told me he got caught cheating on his wife. She didn't know why he lost his job as a trooper – one can only guess.

I was glad I hadn't reported him as many of my friends were suggesting. The Universe – the Angels – must have taken care of the details. His tapestry was being woven in a very humbling way. It wasn't my job to be a part of that.

Chapter 5

After my experience with Marty, I became even more interested in the invisible worlds and my spiritual journey intensified. It was then that my whole life and everything around me changed dramatically.

While the boys were young, I was employed at several part-time jobs. At times I wished I could be more than one person. I taught art classes in my garage and at the Academy of Arts in the next town, Easton, and was a substitute teacher at the St. Michaels elementary school. At the same time I had begun writing and was creating clay sculptures to exhibit. I combined jobs and often read the poetry I had written the night before to my adult art students in my studio. I juggled sitters and preschool to free up time for all these jobs.

For two years I created bronze wildlife sculpture at a foundry. On those days I would drop the boys at the Gibsons' across the street at six in the morning, drive for two and-a-half hours to get to work, making this trip three days a week. Some nights I didn't get home until 10 or 11 o'clock. I had been commissioned to do two life-size bronze Great Blue Herons and was determined to complete them both. It was a dream come true – finally working in bronze after years of clay and plaster. This is what I had gone to art school for. This would make me a *real* artist.

I was on my way back from one of these long days when I had an experience that I could not explain. In those days I was always in a hurry; there wasn't a minute to spare. Everything was done in the same way on each trip. I was on what one might call autopilot. There was the gas station on the way home that I always stopped at to fill up with gasoline and get coffee. Coffee was what kept me going when I physically ran out of gas. I drank a lot of it even though my heart had an unpleasant habit of jumping around and skipping beats. I was pushing myself to the edge without knowing it – the super mom syndrome.

It was pit-stop time. I pulled up by the gas pump and as I opened the door of the car to get out, my heart stopped beating – at least that is what it felt like. As I filled the tank and made the familiar walk into the store to pay, I found myself above my body. I was looking down at myself and having a conversation with myself. "My heart is not beating. I don't look any different. I don't look pale. How can I be walking and looking normal when my heart is not beating?" As usual, I quickly grabbed the key to the restroom as I handed the cashier the money for the gas. Though I didn't feel that I could speak out loud, I seemed to be able to do anything else that I wanted. "I'm glad no one is in line to pay. I don't know how long I can go on like this. I have to go to the bathroom." I went in, sat down, and put my head in my lap. The magical throne, my safety net, would bring me back. "I wonder how long I can go without my heart beating? I hope it starts again soon." As the endless stream of urine came forth, I came back into my body and my heart started to beat once more.

Now I was really confused. As I drove the rest of the way home, I tried to explain what had happened to me. It was impossible for me to not have a heartbeat for so long and yet be able to act and look normal. I had experienced no pain. There was no heart attack. At that time it didn't occur to me that I had been out of my body and that is why it felt as though my heart had stopped beating. This was one of several things that happened around that time that sent me searching for answers.

There were workshops to attend, spiritual books to read, and a meditation group to join in addition to all the other things on my plate. My circle of friends changed and I found that the things I chose to include in my life were also changing. I was writing more and making fewer trips to the foundry. I began to give workshops – not on creating ceramic or bronze sculpture – but on discovering the creative force in one's life. I gave a workshop using the small book that I had written on creativity – *Avatar – You Are The Creator*. I felt more fulfilled creating with words while making objects to set on coffee tables began to have less purpose for me.

The two bronze herons had been completed and were placed in their new homes. I had proven that I could be a *successful artist*. All of the goals I had set for myself from my early childhood were in view but I no longer wanted them. One of the herons was exhibited on several occasions and each time was written up in the paper. It won awards and everyone loved it. The owner of the foundry offered me a partnership and wanted me to move closer to the foundry so I could work full time for him. He offered me the use of his gallery to exhibit and to sell my work. I should have been happy and excited about all of this but I wasn't.

The restlessness within me that had started soon after my husband's sudden departure was always there, whispering in my ear. Those whispers were what kept me questioning everything. I no longer knew what I wanted, who I was, or what my goals were. I did know what I didn't want and that was to work at the foundry. So I gave up what had once been my dream, filled my plate with a quest for understanding, and began sculpting with words.

A very special story now comes to mind. It was Mother's Day, 1988, and Jon was eight years old. He came into my room and asked, "Mommy, can I use your typewriter?" In those days we didn't have a computer and Jon would watch me as Spirit came through to write the poems on the typewriter.

I said, "Of course," and turned over to go back to sleep. A short while later he came back with a tray. There, on the tray, was my special Mother's Day breakfast which consisted of water, Wasa crackers, an apple, and some beautiful dandelions from the back yard. Jon, who was always very responsible, remembered that I was always on a diet and this is what I ate most mornings. He also knew that he mustn't use the stove, or pick the flowers from the garden. Then I noticed a piece of paper with this poem written on it....

You are the key to the treasure
The treasure that lies deep within
That treasure is called LOVE.

At that age, he hadn't mastered spelling or punctuation. I later made those small changes. What was apparent, and so touching, was his love. I asked him, "What made you do such a special thing?" as I cried and hugged him.

He said, "I was just doing what you do and something told me to write those words." It was apparent now that I was living with a young master.

Spiritual studies filled my life and more direct guidance from Spirit created new awareness. I became interested in reincarnation and the possibility we may have had other life times and were learning through them. My spirit guides, as I now called them, taught me how to regress myself through meditation and a form of self-hypnosis.

I discovered memories of other incarnations that helped me understand who my husband may have been, why we were together and why he had to leave me once more. Jon and Mikie were open to these techniques and we had several sessions together. This work seemed to help them deal with some challenging people in their lives. We were making an effort to see from a different perspective. I didn't want the boys to have to live their lives feeling like victims as I had. Part of me wondered if we weren't just making up these stories about other life times. Reincarnation hadn't been proven to me yet. Maybe this was just a creative way of dealing with our lives and our issues.

One day I found myself at a workshop on regression therapy. Unfortunately, I can't recall the name of the women that gave the workshop. Names have, in the past, been difficult for me to remember. The energy of a person is what sticks in my mind – our interactions or the features of their faces. This was a rather large group of about twenty people. It was the first time this woman had been given permission by her spirit guides to teach these techniques to other people. She had asked that only those souls attend who were ready to learn and use this information for the highest good of all. I felt honored to be there.

The work came easily to me so I was asked to use these methods to regress several people that day. Her method was to teach by doing. She would come behind me at different times and touch me. Just her touch would clear any blocks and I could clearly see what to say or do next. I was being taught how to step out of the way and let my soul do the work. At one point, she placed a crystal in my hand and I went into an altered state. I became a clearer channel for the energy that was needed to assist the person to remember. (I still have the crystal. When I am guided to, I use it while doing a regression or *Time Spin* as I now call this work.)

At the end of the day, it was my turn to be regressed and I was a little nervous. In the past I had only regressed myself with the guidance of my angels. It was much easier assisting someone else. When it came time for me to receive I always felt awkward. The owner of the house was a Native American shaman. He and his partner owned a crystal shop and their house was filled to overflowing with crystals. I liked him and he seemed to be a very powerful soul. He offered to work with me on my regression.

In no time at all (slight pun) I was back in the past, walking along a stream in a village. I was a Native American woman with a three year-old son and I was three months pregnant. Next I saw myself sitting in a teepee. A man from another tribe burst in and buried his tomahawk in my back between my shoulder blades. He killed me and my unborn child. My spirit, in shock and anger, stayed trapped between worlds as I watched my three year-old son be kidnapped by the murderer. My son was raised by this man and was told that he was his true father which of course was a lie.

At the end of the process, the shaman doing the regression lifted his ceremonial staff above my body, gathering up all the energy strings from my etheric field that kept me tied to that karma and pain. As he lifted his staff my body also lifted up. I had my eyes closed and wasn't aware of what he was doing. All that remained on the floor was part of my seat. My body, now in a "V" shape, suddenly came crashing back down to the floor as he cut through the air above me severing those energy strands with his staff.

I frequently had pain and discomfort between my shoulder blades. After the regression there was rarely any pain there. I have noticed that when I do feel twinges of discomfort in that area, I am usually dealing with the next level of clearing similar issues. In fact, as I now write these words, that part of my body is speaking to me. It may be that the process of writing about this is allowing the next level of this energy to rise to the surface to be released. At least that is how I have come to explain it.

Once I came back into my body and into this world after the regression, I started to put the pieces of my tapestry together. I had been three months pregnant and the mother of a three year-old when my husband departed in this lifetime. There were a lot of similarities in the two lifetimes. Was this a karmic pay back? Had Pete been the same man who killed me and took my son? Maybe he came back to give my children back to me. Maybe I was to learn to love the man I hated so much, only to lose him after he gave the boys back to me.

During the first months of my pregnancy, I hemorrhaged and spotted frequently. I was sent to bed. Just one week before my husband's accident I stopped bleeding. My doctors thought I had already lost the baby. I wondered if my husband's soul made an agreement to leave, like a trade, so that my son and I could be saved? Was this a Karmic payback – leaving me to grieve for the man I had previously hated. How ironic. Was my Karma learning to love the soul I hated so much for killing me and taking my child and unborn son? Was it just a coincidence that I was 3 months pregnant with a 3 year-old son when my husband died? Isn't it interesting that the heavy bleeding I was experiencing stopped just before the plane crash. Were these all just coincidences?

Another memory surfaced to support my theory. I remembered Pete telling me when we first met that he thought he had been an Indian shaman in a previous lifetime. Whenever I would see spirits in the darkness of our bedroom, as I often did, he would claim that they were only there because he had been a shaman. I thought at the time that he was teasing me. He didn't see anything and probably thought I was just dreaming or delusional. Maybe it was his way of trying to get my attention because he didn't have the ability to see the other dimensions as I sometimes did. After he passed to the other worlds my experiences got more frequent and he wasn't around to take the credit – at least not in the flesh.

This regression assisted in healing some of the pain I was

feeling after Pete's accident. I achieved a feeling of completeness, greater purpose, and a closer connection to Pete, even though he was no longer physically with me.

At the end of the workshop, each of us was asked a simple question, "Who are you?" We had been asked this same question at the beginning of the day. We were to note how this experience had changed our answer. When we introduced ourselves at the beginning of the day it had been easy to answer this question, "I am Joyce Gedeon. I live in St. Michaels with my two children."

Now, after what I had experienced, I hadn't a clue what to say. While waiting and listening to all the wonderful things the others had to say, a queasy feeling filled the pit of my stomach. What could *I* possibly say? Speaking in front of people always terrified me. I wanted to say just the right thing because I wanted so much for everyone to like me. My ego and low self-esteem were overwhelming. When it came my turn, I went blank, and then out of my mouth came these words, "*I am a light being – a soul. I exist in all times and all dimensions simultaneously.*" I had finally discovered who I was. Tears of joy streamed down my face as I acknowledged the truth. I had spoken through my soul's awareness in public for the first time.

The woman who gave the regression workshop told me that I should consider making this my work. I decided to take her advice and became a regression therapist.

Years later I met another shaman – Michael. There was an instant knowing I had been with him in another lifetime. Shortly after meeting him he showed me the portrait of an Indian chief he had created with pastels. I knew it was his self-portrait, even though it didn't look like him now. Before he told me his story of that time, my inner knowing was telling me that we had been together when he was that chief. I had just met Michael minutes before, and had never shared any of my past lives with him.

Michael was now telling me his story, "In a past life I was an Indian chief. My wife was murdered by a shaman from another tribe who had been jealous of my marriage. The other man wanted my wife and young child. He killed my wife and our unborn child, took our son and I never saw him again." He described the murder just as I had remembered it.

I thought to myself, "We have found each other again!" Then I asked him, "Was I your wife in that life time?"

His reply was, "Yes, and I never married again."

Michael and I are still very close. He is like a brother to me. We weren't meant to be married in this life time. He gave me the picture of the Indian chief just before he left to go out West. I have it hanging in my bedroom. Every time I look at it, it reminds me of how interconnected the whole pattern of life and rebirth is. There were just too many coincidences to ignore. I wasn't the only one with the same memory. It was easier to believe the visualizations I had experienced. Now they were real, not just made up stories.

Chapter 6

After only a few hours sleep, I am once again abruptly awakened by a scratching sound on the wall. It is 5 A.M.. There is a loud ringing in my ears and from past experience, I know that this is the time when the writing flows. The children are asleep and the TV is peacefully disconnected.

As I sit at the computer in this quiet house, I am transported back through the eyes of my soul to the spooky old farm house that the boys and I were living in. I see myself being awakened at three in the morning by a loud knocking at the door – with no one there. I get up with a knowing that it is time to work on my second book – *Kingdoms of Light*. My writing is done in a notebook on my lap in the living room using a pencil – not a computer. Digging deeper in time, I look back at the journey, the tapestry that was woven to put us in that house. Standing out in this pattern is the memory of Betty.

My first meeting with Betty occurred in a small park near Alexandria, Virginia, where she lived. I decided to go to the park with another close friend, Orpha, who had been telling me wonderful inspiring things about Betty. On this Sunday, we participated in a guided visualization that Betty gave without charge every week.

There I was in the park, walking up to a large group of people who were already in the middle of a visualization lead by Betty. Orpha and I sat down on the grass quietly trying not to disturb the others. I hadn't even caught my breath when Betty said to the group, "Now go into your heart and see a white rose, a bud still closed. As it opens, smell its beautiful fragrance and have that fragrance fill your entire being." As I took a deep breath, I could actually smell the scent of the rose. I wasn't deep in meditation having just arrived, so I opened my eyes to see if someone had a rose nearby. The smell was so strong – maybe someone was holding a rose under my nose. To my surprise no rose or perfume was in sight. There was nothing visible to explain this strong essence. Later I asked others if they had smelled it. Several said they had but many had not. Betty had gotten my attention.

A few weeks later, Orpha invited me to attend a healing workshop being held at her house in Manassas, Virginia. Since I lived in St. Michaels, Maryland, a three hour drive was involved. Orpha had been attending a weekly meditation group that I was a member of, making that long drive every week for about three months. If Orpha hadn't followed her guidance, making this long journey every week for a two hour meditation, I would never have met Betty and my whole life would have gone in a different direction.

The workshop was well attended. Because Orpha's house was overflowing, I found myself in need of a place to stay for the night. Betty was also taking this workshop. We talked about what had happened the first time that I met her in the park. Orpha suggested that I might stay at Betty's house as she had more room. Betty invited me to come and stay in her condo in Alexandria.

That evening as we sat in her living room, Betty told me her story. She had just liquidated two thriving businesses – an investment counseling service and a subliminal tape business. Before that she had been the vice president of a large insurance company. She had been society's picture of a powerful and successful businesswoman. Betty was in the process of letting go of everything she had accumulated – almost all her material possessions.

That night she introduced me to her philosophy of living. Much of what she was learning to live, she had learned from her teachers, Geoffrey and Diana Bullington. Through Betty I was receiving their teaching, even though I hadn't met them.

We had an instant liking for each other and had a lot of fun talking till the wee hours of the morning. After going to sleep around three o'clock I was awakened. I had become accustomed to being awakened in the middle of the night to write a poem or other material. This time the message I wrote was short and to the point, *"Invite Betty to come and stay with you at your house after the workshop."* I was shocked and promptly went back to sleep. I would share this with her and she could do with it whatever she wanted.

The next morning my mind was busy thinking of all the reasons why Betty shouldn't come to my house. I thought to myself, "My house is a mess. She probably doesn't like children. We hardly know each other. She is too busy with the sale of her condo and all her possessions. She can't just stop everything and for no apparent reason come with me." A part of me doubted that she would choose to come and yet I knew I must deliver the message. What she would do with it was up to her.

"Betty, I got a message last night that you are supposed to come with me to my house when I leave."

She shook her head and immediately said, "No." There was a long pause and she said, "I take that back. I will have to pray about it. I will ask God if that is what I am to do."

I was watching her walk her talk. This was an opportunity for her to practice what she had been teaching her students. She went within to consult with her soul – her God Self. From that higher perspective, she had a better view of the tapestry that was in the process of being created. She had been teaching her students to go within, and without having to know why or how, to trust that guidance and follow it. She did not question the message she received just as I knew not to question giving her what I had gotten. When Betty came out of her room she said, "I don't believe it but my guidance was to go with you."

The day after the workshop was spent getting things in order for the trip. She made phone calls to postpone or cancel appointments. She put her busy life on hold and took off with me on the spur of the moment. We began weaving a new tapestry together.

Chapter 7

As we drove across the Woodrow Wilson Bridge leaving Alexandria, Betty and I were awestruck. There, directly over the bridge, was a huge and very vibrant double rainbow. As we drove under the rainbows they gave us the feeling that even the heavens had affirmed our choice and the journey God was to take us on.

At this time in my life, the concept of *God* represented an external force, and not the understanding of a God that was within and not separate from us. That would come later. This process however was bringing me closer to Source by seeing and communicating with what was always all around me.

For the next two weeks, Betty taught me a new way of living. We would turn to the Creator for guidance in everything we did. We would get up in the morning with no plans and ask God what we should do that day – living in the moment following our guidance without question. Sometimes the guidance came in meditation, sometimes from signs around us. Messages were found on license plates or billboards, or maybe on the side of a truck. Nature played a part as we became keenly aware of whatever caught our attention. Animals and children could also be messengers. We were learning to interpret everything around us as a reflection of our soul communicating to our human awareness. As we worked together to gain this awareness, our tapestries were merging, strengthening, and empowering the weave tenfold.

The game plan was to follow our combined guidance no matter what – always saying a prayer that Geoffrey and Dianna Bullington had given to Betty. I still repeat it many times a day, *"With goodness to all concerned and only Thy will being done."* It was not our intention to have the weave of the tapestry we were creating interfere, harm, or hinder anyone else's.

Living in the moment made the next two weeks fly by. It was as though we had always known each other and yet just met the day before. Linear time had already gotten lost in our tapestry. Betty was guided to go home and I was guided to go with her. The Gibsons across the street watched the boys for a few days and Betty and I headed back to Alexandria.

Betty completed some unfinished business and I helped her with a moving sale. We talked about where we should go from here. The conversation lead to a common desire we shared to have a retreat center. I had been wanting to leave St. Michaels. There were too many memories that kept me in the past. Being around Betty had given me the belief that I could do anything if I had enough faith in God.

Before she had met me, Betty was told by Spirit to start a retreat center in Shenandoah. She had found hundreds acres in the town of Shanandoah. She made an offer and just before the contract would have been accepted two men from Kuwait offered more money and bought it out from under her. It was this land that she wanted me to see. We checked in with the boss – God – and were guided to go to this small town in Virginia the next day.

The farm was located just outside of town on a rise that overlooked the Massanutten mountain range. There was a beautiful view of the mountain with a pond at the entrance. A long gravel driveway wound around past a big barn and the older of two large houses. It then came to a stop in front of a newly renovated house. Both houses were vacant with cow pastures on two sides.

Betty wondered out loud, "Why are these houses still empty? It looks as if the new owners bought them and then did nothing with them. Maybe we can rent them from the new owners while we look for land to build the retreat center?" We drove across the road and found a man working on his car. Rolling down the window Betty asked him, "Do you know anything about the farm across the street that is vacant?"

"I don't know much. The other house is empty too. (The property was divided by a highway and there was yet another empty house on that parcel.) A family was living in that one but they moved out. We haven't seen anyone around. If you call the previous owners maybe they can tell you something."

We thanked the man for his help. That was a great idea. Betty still had their phone number since she had tried to buy their property.

We called and were able to get, the new owner, Mohammed's phone number from them. Without hesitation we were on the phone. The next day we were sitting across from him in Betty's condo in Alexandria. God doesn't waste any time. Things were moving quickly without resistance. This must mean we are heading in the right direction.

Mohammed, who lived on Holy Drive near Washington, D.C., was a quiet man. (We took note of his name and where he lived and saw this as a sign that we were heading in the right direction.) He was tall and had a dark complexion. His quiet manner gave him an air of mystery. He reminded me a little of the man whom I had met in the pub – the one who suddenly appeared in my bed, uninvited. They were both from the same part of the world. Whenever he was asked a question, there was a long pause. Maybe he too was also consulting with a higher authority.

I did most of the talking since I would be the one renting the house. It was important to say just the right thing so I consulted with my spirit guides. The words flowed and as I spoke, I wondered why I was telling him about our spiritual beliefs. Betty and I had agreed to say very little about that, lest he think we were strange. He was a perfect stranger and from another land. We weren't aware of his beliefs and didn't want to offend a possible new landlord. However, there I was blurting out everything, the retreat center, channeling, and of course, doing whatever God told us. I even told him about my circumstances, my husband's accident, my two children and my spiritual quest for understanding. He was also informed as to my very limited funds. I told him that I had a house in St. Michaels with a mortgage that I had put up for sale. He never said a word, just sat expressionless while I went on and on. Every now and then Betty would attempt to quiet me. I knew she was wondering what I was doing.

This wasn't little Joyce talking. Oh, I was in control of and aware of what I was saying, but I was speaking through my soul to his soul. Part of me knew that the actual words really didn't matter. I was coming from the pureness of my heart. I reasoned that if Mohammed didn't respond to that then this wasn't the place for us to set up the center, and he wasn't someone I wanted to do business with. If I didn't hide anything, then there would be less to worry about in the future that might surface. We would be free to explore all possibilities with regard to the center.

There was a very long pause. Betty and I sat without a clue as to what he might say. It seemed like a long time but was probably just minutes. Then this man of few words said, "You may rent the house for $170 a month including the electricity." Betty and I looked at each other and smiled. We had expected a much higher figure, and never dreamed it would include utilities. Then he added, "I only ask that you watch over the other empty house and take care of the property. You won't have to cut the grass as the farmer will do that. He keeps his cows in the barn and pasture. You will live in the older and larger house. From time to time, there may be people who come and stay in the other house. We are planning to build a water bottling factory on the adjacent land and may need to house architects or engineers on occasion. When the other house is empty, you may also have the use of it for your center. Your guests may stay there too."

I asked if we could go and look inside the houses. He gave us the keys to the houses and we agreed to call him as soon as we made a decision. This seemed like a deal I couldn't turn down. It would be a little difficult paying the extra rent but surely my house would sell soon. Then we would be in a position to buy our own land and be more informed about the area we were moving to.

We wasted no time and went back with keys in hand. As we entered the house Mohammed intended for me to live in, Betty hesitated. "I don't want to go inside. I don't have good feelings about this house, Joyce. I would never stay here or even visit you. The energy doesn't feel good." After saying that she quickly went back outside, leaving me standing in what seemed to me to be a great old house. I walked through it and thought it was well worth the rent he was asking. It would need a little paint and some cleaning up but for an old farm house it was great. There was only one room on the second floor that gave me an eerie feeling. When I went inside it was very cold and I got goose bumps all over. In that room which lead to a porch, there was a door that refused to open.

We called Mohammed to tell him of our decision. Since Betty was at that time, an integral part of the retreat center we were planning to create, I felt compelled to say, "I cannot accept your generous offer if it means having to live in the older of the two houses."

He couldn't believe we would turn down his offer. The house had been worth four times that. I told him, "It has nothing to do with money. The energies in the house are not compatible with a retreat center, but we are interested in the other house."

I was learning how to have faith in God and not give in to my fears of lack. Letting go of my lack and limitation allowed the creation to be more than I thought possible – a richer weave. This lesson continues to be something I am relearning all the time; letting go of my control and surrendering to source – God – the God that is within each of us.

There was a long pause on the phone. "I will let you stay there for free." How tempted I was – something for free! But just how free was it if it didn't serve the divine tapestry we were weaving? Everything in me screamed to accept the offer but thanks to Betty's faith in her guidance, I found the courage to again turn him down.

Now he was really perplexed. I guess he had never met anyone like us. I again told him, "It doesn't matter about the money; we have to have the newer house or we will make no deal at all."

Then he said, "If that is your final word, then I must consult with my cousin as he is part owner. I will call you tomorrow with our decision." I was relieved that at least he hadn't said no.

We prayed a lot that night, *"With goodness to all concerned and only thy will being done, allow this house to be ours only if it is in the highest good for all."*

The next day our prayers were answered – this must be a good thing for everyone concerned. Mohammed was on the phone saying, "We have decided to let you live in the newer house." Some kind of miracle I thought. God must have been in communication with Mohammed too!

Since this house was in much better condition I asked, "What will you be charging us to rent this house?"

To my astonishment he replied, "There is no rent. The house is free and I will also pay the electric bill."

He asked if we would clean up and paint the older house for

his friends and the people who may be staying there while the factory was under construction. He would pay us for the work and pay for all materials. He also asked if we would purchase furniture for the house. He would send a check in advance to cover the furniture and painting supplies. Mohammed was aware of the energy in the house and asked if I knew of anyone who could clear it. He also gave us permission to use the house for any guests that we might have at our center when he wasn't using it. Of course I accepted his generous offer. I had a new job fixing up this old house and clearing its energy – ghost busting.

I was convinced that this had to be a message from God. I must leave my house immediately even if it was not yet sold. Betty helped me with a huge garage sale – she was getting to be an expert at this since she had just done the same with her things. I put my house on the market with a different realtor and in the same month that this new journey had started, we moved to Shenandoah, Virginia.

Little did I know just how much this move would change my life. Even though it had been filled with strange happenings, I never could have imagined just how strange it would get. Now that this period of my life has ended, I have a different understanding of what occurred and it doesn't seem outrageous any longer.

It is as though we are tricked into taking a path or making a decision. What we think is the purpose for our action is often just a small detail in a whole pattern of events – events that affect not just us but many others. When we can rise above the pattern we are immersed in, and see through the eyes of our soul, we gain a clearer perspective of our real purpose. From that view, it is easier to see that God has to answer many prayers at the same time to best serve the weave of a universal tapestry. When your prayer is answered, every other prayer has to be answered for the highest good of the total consciousness.

It is as if God is dangling a carrot in front of our noses appealing to what will motivate us – our ego. We grab it and gobble it up. That carrot has a purpose. We may misinterpret that purpose, but your soul knows what motivates you to act, and uses that carrot to guide you in the creation of your tapestry.

The most powerful tool that I would be given in this journey was *faith* – the knowing that God was not separate from me. I could count on this inner knowing and see through my soul the whole picture. This would guide my heart, head, hands and feet in consciously co-creating this Universal Tapestry of Love.

The town denied the zoning for the factory. Only a few of Mohammed's friends came to stay in the other house. We had the use of that newly painted and furnished house whenever we needed it. Although we hadn't planned to stay long, we were there for three years – rent free. It wasn't until the end of the third year, when Mohammed's cousin became sole owner of the property, that we had to pay for the utilities. As for the ghost busting, that is yet another story.

Chapter 8

From the moment we arrived with the moving van, strange things began to occur. Two strong young men, the sons of a good friend, were hired to move our belongings and drive the rented truck to our new home in Shenandoah, Virginia. Jon was in fourth grade and Mike was in first grade. They had never moved their home before so this was a new experience for them. I, on the other hand, had moved so many times my mother said I must have been left on the door step by gypsies.

Everything went without incident. The boys and I were so tired that we slept very soundly and hadn't noticed anything out of the ordinary that night. The two young men who were in sleeping bags on the floor of the downstairs front room had a completely different experience. The next morning they reported getting little or no sleep. One of the two said, "The front door kept opening and closing. The lights were flipping on and off all night long. We would get up and close the door and turn off the lights and a few minutes later have to get up and do it all over again." They also said, "We heard strange noises that couldn't be explained all night and had a lot of cold chills and goose bumps." They were invited for breakfast but turned down the offer and left in a hurry to take the truck back. After wishing us luck in our new home they remarked, "We wouldn't want to live here."

As we settled into our new surroundings, we too, were noticing things that defied explanation. In the mornings we would often find all the lights in the house on and the front door wide open. It became difficult to find anything. Objects would either be moved or completely lost – never to be found again. On many occasions late at night, we could hear drumming coming from the century-old house just a short distance from the one we were now living in.

Since I had promised Mohammed that I would work on the other house I decided to start my spiritual house cleaning there. No one had lived there for some time. The mother of the family that had lived in our residence passed on to the other side while living in that house. When I entered through the back door chills gave me the distinct feeling that spirits were present. My thought was maybe it was the old woman's spirit.

I remembered my first visit to this house and the room upstairs with the strange door that wouldn't open and decided to start there. It had been the place where I had felt the most energy. As I entered the room the temperature dropped at least ten degrees. When I tried to open the door, chills ran up and down my spine and all the hair on my body stood on end. I turned the knob and pulled and tugged and strained but without success. "The door must be nailed shut," I thought to myself. I called to Betty, who had gotten up enough courage to come into the house and was downstairs. "Betty will you come up here and see if you can open this door? It is really stuck."

She came up, walked over to the door, turned the handle, and opened it easily. "There's nothing wrong with this door," she said.

We looked inside and of course there were no bodies, just an empty porch. This left little doubt in my mind that something strange was going on. On several occasions I tried to open that door and was never successful, while other people had no difficulty at all.

Until this time, my only experience communicating with souls on the other side had been with my first boyfriend, Joey, and my husband Pete. I didn't know enough to feel comfortable with the unknown spirits of this place and didn't have a good feeling about it. There was plenty of spiritual house cleaning to keep me busy where we were living, and it didn't feel as intense, so we stayed out of the old house for a while.

Strange things continued to occur in our new house, to us and to our pets. We had two dogs. Mindy, a mixed breed was a little mop of long golden hair. Star was a black lab puppy, who was about six months old. They slept at the foot of my bed and every morning would awaken me with their cold noses announcing their desire to go out. I would dutifully get up and stumble down a flight of stairs to the front door and let them out. As the ritual began one morning, I was awakened by Star licking my hand that was hanging over the edge of the bed. I got up, went down the stairs, eyes half shut, and opened the front door. First came Star as always, big, black, and full of puppy. Then came little Mindy taking her time as she was much older. I went to close the door thinking they were both outside when another big black dog brushed by my leg and ran out the door at the last minute. Now my eyes were opened quite wide and I immediately followed outside to see who the third dog had been. Of course there were only two dogs, Star and Mindy, in our fenced front yard. Now we were dealing with spirits from the animal world too! Until this time I had never thought about the possibility of a spirit world for animals.

Early one morning, around two or three I went downstairs to write. This was the only time when it was quiet in our house. As I sat in the living room waiting to hear words to write, the love seat suddenly started to shake. It then lifted up off the floor several feet, and shook violently. This really caught my attention. I have never been a small person, and to my surprise, the end of the sofa that my largest part was on lifted up first. As was the case when anything interfered with my writing, I got very annoyed. Because I was in the moment, there hadn't been time for fear to take hold but I was angry. This was the last straw. I knew it was time to set this spirit free. I was determined that no soul, dis-embodied or otherwise, was going to scare me out of this free and beautiful place.

On many occasions, attempts were made by me and many others to have the disruptive energies cleared, but to no avail. My sons decided to share my bed at night. They were getting spooked too and didn't want to sleep alone. I couldn't blame them and before long, on any given night, I would awaken to two boys, two dogs, and oh yes, our two cats – all in bed with me. Good thing I had a king-size bed. Even then it proved a bit too much at times.

My friends, many of whom were spiritual healers or teachers, began to come to the center. They often came to find rest and peace – a chance to focus on healing themselves. A name was chosen – Crystal Rainbow Center. A weekly meditation group formed and yoga classes were held every week in the living room. A healer named Samuel became a permanent boarder on weekends. He saw clients and did exchanges with me to pay for his rent.

Samuel was a Reiki master, among other things, and had agreed to give the Reiki empowerments to me for room and board. I was very interested in this ancient healing art and many of the other healing tools and techniques Samuel might teach me, so I was most happy to have him with us. The house was big; even with the extra boarder, we still had room for guests and a separate room that we called the meditation room. It was there we would go to talk to our guides, pray, or channel, receiving guidance and information. Samuel had been a very serious student and teacher of metaphysics. I, on the other hand, was just a novice.

Living in the middle of this new center was my young family. Giving time and equal attention to everyone was challenging but then that is what I have always thrived on. Because I was so busy clearing unwanted spirits, setting up a center, learning about metaphysics, taking care of my family, and breaking ground for a large organic garden, I hadn't noticed how lonely Mikie had been. He felt the loss of his playmates the most.

He came to me one day after Samuel and I had once again attempted to rid the house of the unwanted spooks and said, "Mom, please don't get rid of the spirits. They are my friends. I like them and if you send them away, I won't have anyone to play with." To say that Mike was a bit strange was an understatement, but in our house strange was normal, so this did not surprise me. I remembered my early experiences with the spirit world and didn't want to do to him what had been done to me. No one ever believed what I was seeing. It was important to allow him to stay open and feel supported by me.

Early in his life, Mike's close connection to the spirit world was obvious. When he was about a year old and just learning to speak, I noticed him staring at a specific part of the room. It was three in the afternoon and nap time. He had just finished his bottle and was dozing off to sleep in my arms when his eyes went suddenly wide open and he pushed himself up in my lap. He sat staring at the center of the archway in the middle of the house. It was obvious he was staring at something that had startled him but there didn't appear to be anything in the room.

Mike knew what his father looked like. I would often talk to the boys about their father while holding his picture. I didn't want them to feel fatherless so I had pictures of Pete around the house. My oldest son, Jon, was three when his father passed. Because he was so young I didn't want him to lose what little memory he had of his dad. Mike, who hadn't been born yet when his daddy left, only had the pictures to make a connection. When I asked Mike what he was staring at in the middle of the room he said, "Da Da," for the first time. It was extremely difficult for me in those days. The hardest part was not dealing with my loss, but having to witness the tragedy of their loss.

For weeks, every day at nap time, Mike would see his father in the same location. I stopped trying to get him to sleep and let him down off my lap to go and sit in the archway to play with his dad. I watched as he engaged in what to me looked like one- sided conversations, knowing this was his way of getting to know his father.

Around age three, Mikie came to me and said, "Mommy, when I was in your belly, Daddy came and told me he had to leave but he loved me."

Later, on a field trip, Mike's preschool visited an antique boat that was moored at the museum where his father had worked. I had accompanied the class, teachers, and several other parents on the tour of the vessel. The man who was giving the tour asked the children if they could identify various objects on the boat. As he pointed to different things he would ask, "What might the sailors of this ship use this for?" Some of the things were easy to guess and others were hard even for an expert. Mike seemed to know the name and purpose of everything on the ship. At four years of age, he knew things that I had never told him. The man was quite impressed with Mike and in an effort to stump him, he had saved the most difficult thing to identify for last. Pointing to a bucket of sand that sat on the deck the man said, "I don't think you know what this is. No one has ever guessed its use."

Mike just smiled and said, "It's a fire extinguisher." The man ended the tour without saying another word. Mike had really surprised the man and he had surprised me too. I had no idea how he knew so much about antique sailing vessels. When I asked Mike how he had all the right answers he said, "My daddy told me. He taught me all about boats." It all made sense. His father had been the curator of the maritime museum and old boats were his passion.

Getting back to the haunted house in Shenandoah – I had come to respect Mike and his connections to the invisible worlds.

On many occasions I would seek his advice on spiritual matters. So I asked him what he knew about the spirits – his new friends.

"There are several spirits in this house, Mom. My two friends are Native American boys. They have a black dog with green eyes. We play with him too. (Was that extra dog I let out one morning?) Then there is the grouchy old man who lives in the basement. He fell off his horse and is still angry about it. My friends are the ones who sometimes turn on the lights. They want me to get up and play. They like to play hide-and-seek with our things too. I have told them that you were getting angry about that so they don't do it as much anymore."

Mike offered to talk to the children and tell them they could stay if they would keep the grouchy old man in the basement. The spirit boys had to promise to stop all their pranks. This proved successful for a while, but the older spirit in the basement, who had lifted and shook me while I was seated on the sofa, wouldn't agree to stay in the basement. We had tried to get him to go into the light but he wanted no part of that. Unless a soul is willing this won't happen. Then I had an idea. What if we offered him a house full of other disembodied souls to be with? We told him about the house next door and helped him find it. Something about the other house must have appealed to him; maybe it was the peace and quiet – not having to deal with meddling people on the other side of where he was. Whatever it was, it worked, and we never had any more trouble from him. The two boy spirits started to behave and Mike still had his new friends to play with.

While talking with Mike, we determined that the drumming

sounds that were coming from the other house were only natural. His playmates told him that this was the spiritual gathering place and ceremonial ground for their people. Things started to make more sense to me. It was no accident that we were guided to this spot.

The Crystal Rainbow Center was established. We had made new friends in the spirit world and made peace with those who had been resistant to our presence. The stage was set and our journeys into the other worlds had just begun.

Chapter 9

I had been seeing for some time, on the ceiling as I lay in bed at night, what I then called space ships. It was difficult for me to understand why I was seeing what appeared to be huge vehicles floating in a small room. I asked a friend, who said he had been abducted by aliens, what he thought about my experiences. I wanted to find out why I was seeing them. Since we had moved to the farm house in Shenandoah, the incidents had increased and I desired a clearer understanding of what this was about. This friend asked me what my earliest vision had been and of course I told him about the snowman. He suggested I regress myself back to that time. Because of his personal experience he was of the opinion that I must have blocked some terrible memory. He thought the regression would release me from some suppressed fear and bring back my memory of what had happened.

Taking his advice, I went into meditation one evening, calling on my spirit guides. I asked to go back to the night that I saw the snowman when I was four years old. I saw the picture of a little girl sleeping in her bed with a large teddy bear next to her. The spirit of the child left her body, still holding her teddy bear. She traveled on a rainbow beam of light. It took her to one of the light vehicles I had recently seen in my room. Inside the vehicle my focus shifted. I was no longer viewing the scene but was inside it

– seeing through the eyes of my soul. There was a circle of light beings dressed in long white robes with hoods and I stood in the middle of the circle. They communicated telepathically, "We are called the Brotherhood of The Light. You are one of us. We are always with you. You may call on us for guidance and protection. When you are older, you will remember this and it will assist you in fulfilling your purpose for this lifetime on earth." Then I shifted back to viewing the scene and saw myself with my teddy bear floating back down the rainbow light to my physical body. All I was allowed to remember at that time was the snowman who helped me get back into my body.

Later, still wanting to know more, I went into meditation again and asked to be reunited with these light beings. This time I found my adult self on the light ship surrounded by the Brotherhood once more. Their hoods were large and it was difficult to see them so I projected the thought, "May I see your faces?" Their response was to remove their robes. Now I could clearly see these beings of light. The golden white light that surrounded and filled them was beautiful and gave me a feeling of great love. They were so luminous that they were almost too bright to stare at. These were not the grotesque beings who had abducted and experimented on my friend. Their form was basically humanoid, with large, beautiful blue eyes, tiny noses and small mouths. They seemed tall but then they weren't standing; they were hovering around me. I knew that I had nothing to fear and felt safe and secure with them. They told me of my purpose for incarnating on the planet at this time.

I started writing and communicating with them regularly. I

wrote a book and was given the title, *Kingdoms of Light*. Although I had no formal training in writing, I found myself now writing poetry. I had been a poor English student. I was left-handed and my handwriting as well as my ability to spell had always been a weak point. There was no enjoyment for me in writing, but when I entered into these altered states of awareness, it became difficult to put the pen down and the words just seemed to flow. In a short time many pages would be completed with little to be altered.

After writing I always feel energized and at peace. Writing has become something I have to do because I love doing it. It is as though I merge with the Creator and become a co-creator consciously in the third dimension. This energy is infused into every cell, every molecule, and every atom of my body. No wonder I've become addicted to writing.

The following is a passage from *Kingdoms of Light*. The poem is one of my favorites. When we moved to Shenandoah, I was instructed not to read any more spiritual material. My guides wanted me to be self-taught through them. As I wrote I learned. I was, however, guided to sleep with select books under my bed but never to open or read them while I was writing *Kingdoms of Light*. In this way, my thinking mind would not interfere with the process of bringing the information through from within. This is what I wrote on December, 17, 1992, from 2:12 a.m. to 4:06 a.m.

It is very early or should I say, late. Who could find the silence with two small boys a-fighting, three cats a-mewing, two dogs a-barking, two birds a-squawking and a hamster running on a wheel, when the sun is up? Someday maybe I will find the silence in the daylight; for right now, which is all we truly have, I find it when the moon is my silent companion. It is in the silence that I hear the whispers ringing in my ears – whispers that a scream can't muffle – talking to me now through all time and creation.

JUST BE STILL AND LISTEN

In the silence hear the whispers,
Sometimes deafening to your ears
Whispers which a scream can't muffle.
Whispers ringing in your ears.

Vibrating now through all eternity,
In the mist of all that is.
Vibrating now throughout the universe.
This your link to all that is.

So in the midst of all the clamor,
Set aside some quiet times,
Just to be still and listen,
That you may hear life's eternal chimes.

We once again greet you dearest daughter. Even though we address you as though you are a separate being, as though we are found outside your consciousness, you know that this is an illusion. Truly, you create the words that seem to be coming to you from an outer source. You are manifesting those words. You are hearing them being spoken to you, but they do not come from outside your being. They come from within your seed of light.

When you gain the awareness that you are ONE and ONE IS ALL, then it will be easier to comprehend this. Nothing is separate or outside of you. What seems to be coming from above is in true reality coming from within. We are within you and you are within us.

You may be saying to yourself, "How could it be both ways. How could you be so huge above me one moment, and so tiny within me the next?" We say to you that we exist only in your perception of where you create us to exist. If you see yourself in the Macro Cosmic Kingdom of Light, you have the one perspective of our place in creation. If your awareness is in the Micro Cosmic Kingdom of Light, we exist for you from another perspective.

So it is that we exist where ever you exist. If your consciousness is in the ALL TIME, then you know that we are you, and you and all creation, exist simultaneously in the NOW. You are us and we abide within and without you and everything that ever was, or is, or shall be.

One may say that the being, Joyce Gedeon, whose awareness in the moment is in the Earth's Physical Kingdom, is receiving this information from the heavens. It is also that when the awareness of Joyce Gedeon is that which is in the Kingdom of ALL TIME − in the Oneness − she is the source, the creator, the manifester of every word and thought that is contained in this manuscript. It is in this kingdom of reality that we exist within her seed of light, and are truly made manifest by her very existence.

We say to you, proclaim your divine right to possess the powers of the Universe by affirming this:

"I am the Source.

I am the Creator.

I am the manifester of oneness

In the ALL TIME."

Proclaim these words and embrace them at all levels of your being, and in so doing, you travel out of Earth's Physical Kingdom to the awareness of the many other kingdoms of being. To travel in these many kingdoms one must give up the idea of going out of the body to arrive at your destination – wherever in creation that may be. When you truly see yourself as the creator – the manifester – you will know that all exists within your very own seed of light. One need only travel within, to arrive at any destination, in any kingdom, at any time. Why travel so far away when the keys to unlocking those doorways – the secrets – lie within the very depths of your own awareness?

When one can truly understand this concept at all levels – when one can feel it, not just think it – it is then that one is truly in the flow of the Wave of ONENESS. It is then that one may begin to create that wave.

We say to you, see yourself riding on the crest of the wave of all creation in the Oneness and the All Time; and then go within and see yourself as the creator of that wave that you are riding.

Have you ever positioned two mirrors facing each other, and sat between them? If you have, you know that what you see is a never ending, infinite series of one mirror inside another mirror.

Each mirror is mirroring itself. If you sit within just one of those mirrors you are in all of those mirrors. In the first mirror you appear huge and in the last, microscopic.

When one stands in the very first doorway, unlocks that very first door, and steps into the mirror of that doorway – it is in that moment, the secrets of the universe are revealed. It is in that moment that one sees reflected from within all creation, that each doorway is contained within the next. There is nothing that exists outside the oneness. There is nothing that truly exists outside your awareness.

Look at yourself in that same mirror. As you move your arm, see yourself in all those other mirrors (doorways), moving in exactly the same way. Ask yourself which reflection is creating this movement, which is the creator, the manifester? Is it the being one can barely make out, way at the end of all the doorways or corridors of your existence; or is it the largest being in the very first doorway, that leads to all the others?

When you realize you are standing in all the doorways simultaneously, that you manifest and create all that is – it is then that you become one with the manifestation you create. You are the wave. You become the golden fluid or liquid light that flows in all the universes. Yes, you are flowing within the seas of awareness and oneness, and at the same time, you are holding those seas in your hand.

So see yourself as the creator of those seas, and in the All Time, see yourself as every tiny particle of light contained and flowing within those seas of light. Say to yourself:

"I am a manifestation of my own creation.
I am one in the eternal seas of all creation.
I am flowing effortlessly through all time in all kingdoms of light
As they are made manifest by me.
I am the loving power of the universes."

The book was completed and I self-published it. I used it to give many workshops. It had been my teacher and now I would use it to teach others.

Chapter 10

The intention of this book isn't just to tell stories. This book is about the message those stories convey. The events weave a pattern that isn't that unique, yet at times, may seem miraculous and synchronistic. The pattern is teaching one how to live in a state of *Grace*. With that in mind, I shall tell another story.

This morning when I woke up, Samuel came to mind. I hadn't thought of him for some time. When I went to the mailbox, something told me a communication from him would be there. There was a magazine from Pagosa Springs, Colorado, in the box. My friend, Samuel, who stayed with us at the center in Shenandoah had moved there. As I opened the magazine I got a message from within – *Samuel has written an article that is inside.* I quickly flipped through the pages, looking only at the authors' names. Sure enough, toward the back, was Samuel's article. Why was I surprised? I was so happy for him. He was being heard. All his hard work must be paying off.

When I came back to continue writing this manuscript, I found out why I had received that particular magazine at that moment. The next entry was about guess who, Samuel. It had been at least three years since I had heard anything from him or about him. We had lost touch because he moved so far away. Now just as I am putting this particular story into the book, I get a magazine that

I haven't even subscribed to with his article in it. That's *synchronicity!*

We travel back in time and space to the Crystal Rainbow Center. Samuel is my teacher. He is a serious, devout and caring light worker. He spends many hours working on his studies – reading, channeling, meditating, and teaching. There was just one little thing that he could not master – seeing the other worlds. More than anything he wanted to be able to see into the other dimensions. As knowledgeable as he was, this aspect still eluded him. I honored his knowledge and dedication and was thankful to have him at the center to teach me. You might say I put him on a pedestal; one that he hadn't asked to be put on.

Samuel knew that Mike and I could see the other dimensions. This must have perplexed him. He was after all *my* teacher, yet he didn't have the gift of sight. He must have wondered why this child and a woman who had read no major spiritual or metaphysical books had been given this gift; and he who had worked and studied so hard, had not.

When we first met Samuel, we were still living in St. Michaels. Orpha introduced me to him. He had been staying at her house doing what he called Empowerments. Orpha suggested that I work with Samuel and get an Empowerment. I did and was very impressed. While he worked on me, I had out-of-body experiences and had visions that assisted me in dealing with my father's imminent passing. I invited him to come to my home and set up appointments for him with my circle of friends. Betty also knew Samuel and on this particular occasion, she was also staying at my home. It was just before our move to Shenandoah.

We were all gathered around the dining room table one evening when Betty asked Mike if he had seen his guardian angel. "Of course," he said.

"What does he look like?" Betty asked.

"He's big and blue and carries a sword and a large shield."

Betty replied, "Angels don't carry swords."

Just then Samuel reached into his brief case and pulled out a card. On the card was a picture of Archangel Michael. It had been painted by Nanette Crist, who said she had been visited by the masters and angels who posed for her paintings. Mike and Betty had never seen the card. The picture was exactly as Mike had described his angel – sword and shield in hand.

Then without being asked Mike said, "I see something right now. There is a man standing behind Samuel. He has blond hair and blue eyes. He has a beard and is wearing a white robe."

Samuel reached into his bag again and pulled out another picture by Nanette Crist. He showed it to Mike and asked, "Is this the man you see."

Mike looked behind Samuel and then looked back at the card – comparing the two. "Yes. That's him."

Later that evening my friend Pat, who led our weekly meditation group, offered to channel for us. She was an in-body channel, meaning other energy beings would speak through her body as her consciousness stepped aside and let them come through her. We had all prepared serious questions to ask her – some pertaining to the fate of the planet and earth shifts. When it came time for

Samuel to ask his questions, in the midst of all this serious talk he said, "Did Mike really see Jesus standing behind me this afternoon?"

The answer was, "Yes and he sees much more."

That was Samuel's introduction to Mike.

When we moved to the center in Virginia, I invited Samuel to stay on weekends. I continued to help him get clients. I was awakening at a rapid rate and since my teacher was good at his job, the student was becoming the teacher too. As I wrote and channeled almost on a daily basis, the visions increased. Almost every night as I lay in bed, the ceiling would open up to reveal the cosmos. Stars, galaxies, geometric shapes, and light vehicles would appear before me. Rainbow discs of light would fill the room. In the morning I would be so excited about what I had experienced the night before I could hardly wait to tell Samuel all about it.

I remember one morning in particular. I was at the kitchen table drawing the light ship that I had seen the night before. Mike, who was now about eight years old, came downstairs and was looking over my shoulder helping me to complete the picture. He said, "Mom, I was on that ship with you last night. I remember what it looked like." As we drew the picture together he continued, "We went to Egypt, to the time of the Pharaohs. They were mistreating the slaves. So we talked to the Pharaoh and asked him to be nicer to them."

Just about that time Samuel came into the kitchen. He had overheard part of our conversation and asked what we were talking about. I showed him the picture we had drawn. He immediately ran upstairs and got a book, *The Keys of Enoch, a* very heavy, complicated, left brained, scientific, metaphysical book he had been studying. This was a book which Mike and I had never seen. Samuel put the book down in front of us on the table and opened it. The page revealed a picture that was almost identical to the one we had just drawn. We were all amazed.

I asked if I could look in the book to find a written description of the ship. Samuel assured me that the book was beyond my simple comprehension. I looked anyway. In just minutes I found what we needed. I said, "This isn't so complicated. It says here that this is the light vessel Archangel Michael and Metatron travel in to teach students." Just days before Samuel and I had been saying prayers, in the meditation room we he had created, asking for guidance and help from guess who – Archangel Michael and Metatron. I borrowed this book and slept with it under my bed. As I did things got clearer and clearer.

I learned a lot from Samuel. I wonder if he ever knew the greatest lesson he taught me, or if he has learned it himself. I haven't seen him for years, so I have no way of knowing how he has evolved as a soul. I do know that the lesson I learned from him was lighten up, have fun and see as the innocent child sees – clearly, without the illusion of separateness to cloud one's vision.

Chapter 11

My faith was tested on many occasions and so was my mother's faith in me. When visiting her one day, she made it quite clear what she thought about my moving to Virginia and writing a spiritual book.

I knew that my mother loved me and her concerns were only for my well-being. She saw me living on the edge of what was deemed acceptable to most normal people. I believe she knew I had always been this way and was concerned about me. The idea of me living so far away from her may not have appealed to her either. She had always lived within a twenty mile radius of the house where she was born and never traveled out of the state. The farthest she had ever gone was Ocean City, Maryland, which is only a few hours away.

She was alone, without a husband for the first time in her life, and so was I. She must have been worried about me moving to a strange place by myself.

My mother is very generous and caring. She is also very outspoken and direct when it comes to expressing her beliefs or opinions. I thank her for giving me those gifts. Without them I couldn't write this book. On this day, she was expressing, in a generous way, just what she thought about what I was doing with my life. We had a discussion about the guidance I was receiving. She asked, "How can you be so sure about what you are hearing? Maybe it is just your vivid imagination?" I didn't know how to explain it in a way that she would understand. How could anyone who hadn't experienced what I had understand?

As we were going to the store she started questioning me again, "Why can't you just be normal like your brother?"

While she was going on about her fears and concerns, I was listening to my inner guidance. I heard, "*Trust your guidance.*" I said, "Mom I'm getting a message right now – *we will find a parking space right in front of the store.*"

My mother said, "That's not possible. It's Saturday and there is never a spot in front at this store." As we got closer to the store I could see a spot in front. It was about two blocks away.

Mom said, "Oh, that doesn't prove anything. Somebody just pulled out. You were just lucky."

Maybe she was right I thought to myself. Then I was guided to tell her, "*In that parking place there will be money on the ground.*" I didn't even know how this had come out of my mouth. It was as though someone else were speaking through me. I was praying it was true because I knew if we found no money, she would never let me forget it. Sure enough as we got closer, about one hundred yards away, just in sight, we saw a bill on the ground.

Now my mother was getting a bit nervous. Again she said, "So what, that doesn't prove anything."

We were too far from the money to be able to see how much was there. Then, to my disbelief, I blurted out, "I'm being told – *it is a twenty dollar bill.*"

My mother said, "That's impossible. How can you see that far? It's probably just a one dollar bill."

I prayed again and quickly pulled into the parking space. I opened the car door, reached down and picked up, guess what, a twenty dollar bill. For the first time in my life I actually saw my mother speechless. Even I was amazed but relieved. My inner guidance had come through.

I hadn't really done this to upset or worry my mother. It just happened before I knew it. It was almost as if I was having my faith confirmed as well.

A short time later we were reminded of this incident. I had run out of cash while visiting her so I wrote her a check for twenty dollars. Mom went upstairs to get me the money and returned with a twenty dollar bill. As she was handing me the bill, we both noticed at the same time that this bill had a rainbow drawn over the pyramid, and the words, Crystal Rainbow Connection, were plainly written above it. My mother said immediately, "It doesn't mean anything!" What a coincidence; the center I was moving to was called the Crystal Rainbow Center. We had just had an argument about my moving there when we found the first twenty dollar bill in the parking lot. I just smiled at her and didn't say a word.

My mom and I had struggled in our relationship, maybe because we were so much alike. What I discovered well after this part of the tapestry was woven gave me many answers about our relationship and why it had been so difficult. That is why I have decided to inject a story from the future about her last days in the physical body.

Mom was rushed to the hospital after her colon ruptured. She was given drugs that caused her to enter a psychotic state. As she was recovering from this experience, she shared things with me that she had been unable to in the past. The event for her and for me was a quantum opportunity for growth.

"You won't believe where I have been," she said. In the past I wasn't allowed to touch her feet, which were swollen and tender from diabetes. Now she asked, "Would you rub my feet?" For the first time in my life I was being honored and my healing abilities were desired by my mother. She had in the past always been fearful of anything that I might be studying; Reiki, Foot Reflexology, Past Life Regressions. She certainly didn't want any of that New Age stuff or alternative healing to even be spoken of. I learned not to go to that area in our conversations. Now she was telling the doctors who came into the room what a gifted healer I was! One good looking doc really got an earful of all my accomplishments. She even invited him to have a seat and experience my foot massage first hand. It was a little embarrassing as she was obviously match making.

This was so uncharacteristic of my mother. It was clear she was not the same person I had known. This was the mom I had always longed for. I had a new friend. We talked for days about things from the past and much healing was happening for both of us. She told me one story that helped me understand why she had been so fearful for me.

Soon after the snowman visited me, my parents fixed a beautiful room up just for me. It was in the attic. The wallpaper had roses all over it and there was a window seat where I could sit and play. Any little girl would have loved the room – any little girl but *me*.

"Why didn't they put that screaming baby in the attic? Why did I have to be the one to move?" I would ask myself. I felt very alone and abandoned – separate from everyone and everything that was safe downstairs.

As I lay in bed at night, the roses on the wall paper would move and I would find myself above the house. Because I didn't understand what was happening and I was afraid, I would go downstairs and try to get in bed with my parents. I refused to stay in the new room. On one occasion, I went outside and down the street in the middle of the night to Joey's house because my parents wouldn't let me in their room. My parents had no choice but to put a lock on the door at the bottom of the stairs.

Many nights because of my fear, I would sleep in front of the door on my teddy bear – my security. When my mom would unlock the door she would find me still asleep on the bottom step with Teddy.

My mother shared with me what happened on one of those nights, "I was seated at the dressing table brushing my hair. You and your brother had been put to bed and your door was locked so I didn't have to worry that you would run off in the night. Just as I was ready to climb into bed with your father, something told me to turn and look. To my shock and surprise you were standing there looking at me. We checked your room. The door was still locked and you were asleep on your teddy at the bottom of the stairs. I never forgot. I was so fearful for you. I knew you were not like most children and I had my hands full protecting you from the world."

I had gone home from the hospital because my mother was doing well. Then they gave her the same drug that caused her psychotic episode before. When that mistake was cleared up and she came back to consciousness, she called me on the phone and said, "I'm back! Honey I'd tell you I love you but how could you believe me after the way I have treated you your whole life?"

"I said I love you mom and I understand." My brother came on the phone then.

Those were the last words she ever said to me. Before I could get back to the hospital, she experienced a stroke to her brain stem and slipped into a coma. In two weeks she was on the other side with my dad. Before she left she had given me her greatest gift – acceptance, understanding, and an apology.

On another occasion I was taught the importance of following my guidance as I had done with my mom when the twenty dollar bill manifested.

Betty often stayed with us at the center. Mike, Betty, and I were going to Harrisonburg to do some shopping at the mall. Just before we reached the town an ambulance pulled in front of us. It's lights were not flashing and it was going very slow. It felt strange to be behind an ambulance and have the desire to pass it. I wasn't sure what to do so I went within and asked. The message was, *"Don't pass . Stay right where you are and follow the ambulance."* Trusting my guidance I did what I heard. My logical mind was thinking, "Maybe we are to send love and light to the person in the ambulance to help them in some way." So Betty and I said prayers and sent Reiki healing energy to the person in the ambulance.

The roads were wet because it had been raining and we were nearing the turn to go to the mall. Because we were so close to the back of this very large tall vehicle, I couldn't see that the traffic light had just turned red. As the ambulance stopped, I was forced to put on the breaks a little faster than I would have desired on these wet roads. However, we managed to stop with at least three or four feet still between my tiny Nissan's bumper and the very thick, high bumper of the rescue vehicle in front of us.

Because of the quick stop we had just made, I looked in my rear view mirror at the car behind us and said a quick prayer. There in the mirror was a rather large car. It may have been a Cadillac. The driver didn't even attempt to stop! Suddenly we were hit from behind and pushed directly into the back of the ambulance. I had on my seat belt and was not hurt. Betty was not wearing hers and was thrown into the dash, and Mike, who was also not buckled up, was thrown into the headrest of Betty's seat. Even though they were thrown around in the car, no one was hurt.

I looked in front of us and could see that the thick, heavy bumper of the ambulance was pushed in considerably. Then my glance turned to the car behind us. The front of this car was smashed in much more than the rescue vehicle but the woman who was driving the car opened her door and got out. She also seemed physically all right.

There was a wide median in the middle of this two-lane

divided highway. I got out of my car but I was afraid to look at it. Instead I was guided to go to the other driver and hug her. She was in tears. Knowing she had caused the accident, she broke down right there in my arms in the middle of the highway. Trying to calm her down I assured her that everyone was alright and the insurance would surely cover the damages. Her daughter, who had been following in the car behind her, joined us. She explained that they were on their way to the hospital to see her father for the last time. He was suffering with cancer and was ready to make his transition.

As we talked, I learned that the woman who hit my car was about to lose her husband of many years and was already in tears before the accident. She was so caught up in her anguish she didn't even see that my car had stopped in front of her.

Realizing the situation, my focus shifted, and the words came through me as I counseled this woman. I told her about my husband and the plane crash. By sharing my experience, I was able to help her to let go of her beloved. I explained that he would be even closer to her even though his physical presence may not be beside her. We stood there in the rain and the three of us prayed for his release from his physical body and his suffering. She calmed down and thanked me for helping her. Then we discovered we were neighbors. They lived just in front of the farm we had moved to. Was this just a coincidence? – Or were we put in just the right place at just the right time?

It was now time to look at the damage. I walked to the ambulance first. Their oversized bumper would have to be replaced as it was pushed into the doors that opened on the back of the van. I turned and looked at the front of my car and to my astonishment there was no damage! My bumper wasn't even dented in. How could this be? Then I went around to the back end; surely there would be damage there. I could see that my neighbor's car needed major repairs. Her grill was smashed in along with her bumper and the hood was pushed up. As I stood in front of her car, I turned and looked down at the rear of my little Nissan hatchback. I couldn't believe my eyes, there appeared to be no damage; not even a scratch. My tiny car, which had been sandwiched between this big rescue vehicle and a much larger car, had no damage at all. How could this be?

The rescue workers came to check each of us to make sure we had no injuries. One of them explained that they had been driving slowly because they didn't want to shake up the woman who was inside the ambulance. She was having a heart attack. They were amazed that she was actually doing better in spite of the accident. I wondered what would have happened if my car had not been there to buffer the impact of the larger car that didn't stop.

A policeman had arrived almost immediately after the accident. He was standing there as I counseled the driver of the other car and did not interrupt us until she had calmed down. Then he questioned each of us about what had happened. He asked her for her license and registration card. Suddenly I realized I had forgotten mine. I had just gotten my new registration card and didn't have it with me. Then I realized that I didn't even have my license. It was in a different purse that had accidentally been left at home. Surely he would give me a ticket for that. I started to pray, "Please God don't let him give me a ticket."

To my surprise he never asked to see my identification. He just told me to take my car to the shop to make sure that there was no hidden damage. Both he and the people in the rescue vehicle were amazed that my car was spared even the slightest scratch. The next day I followed his advice and took my car in to be checked. The mechanic told me that there was no damage, not even a loose muffler.

I was glad that I had faith in and listened to Spirit. The accident taught me that God makes miracles out of what some may see as misfortune. Another important lesson was that when living in the moment, and following without question your inner voice, one never knows where it may lead. The important thing is to have faith that whatever may happen, it is in the highest good for you as well as all concerned. When one learns to live in this state of grace, miracles become an everyday occurrence. It is then one understands that *Miracles are just a burst of faith.*

Chapter 12

Hello world! I am in the future where the Crystal Rainbow Center is but a memory. My boys have become young men and much has happened that I have yet to write about.

This morning finds me completely isolated from all electrical power. We have been graced with a beautiful, heavy blanket of snow. My dream catcher trees that surround the house are so thickly covered with snow there appears to be a dense white forest around me. It is a beautiful fairy landscape. About six inches have fallen and the forecast predicts snow continuing throughout the day.

I'm glad that I gathered dry wood for the fire. With no electricity it has become our only source of heat. The boys went skiing last night (we now live near a popular ski resort) and didn't make it home before the snow, so I'm all alone in this white crystal fairyland.

The birds have gathered on my deck to feed on seed and suet cakes. There is one large red headed woodpecker who I feel I know personally. He comes every day and rests on the rail of the deck. He is patient, as he watches the other smaller birds take their turns pecking at the suet cake. He is so large he could easily overpower the others, but he just waits for an opening, and then he flies to the suet which is hung from a delicate netted bag. He hangs upside down with his tail feathers curled under, and swings in the air as he pecks at the seeds encased in fat.

He falls off and hits the deck with a plunk. He isn't hurt; just shaken up a bit. I guess even though birds can fly, if they are caught by surprise, they too can fall. This reminds me of that saying, "Even the mighty may fall." Nature is speaking to me as I hear the words of a poem:

REMEMBER

In this silent moment,
Suspended in the pure white of snow-tufted space,
I listen for the words of truth,
That sustain my faith.

Cast adrift from the heavens,
This tiny planet spins.
Its fallen angels struggle,
To survive within its midst.

We, all of us, have fallen,
Tho' winged that we were,
From great heights of power,
To this humbling planet's woe.

Though our souls, they may be tortured,
Yet still alive within,
The memory of God's sweet kiss,
Remains upon our lips.

God's heart is always open,
To every single soul.
Even if we have forgotten,
How God loves us so.

It is in faith we struggle,
To be free from the night.
This faith sustains our power,
To once again unite.

To fly again as angels,
With wings of feathered white.
All fallen ones shall once again,
Find truth within God's sight.

And so my fellow journeyers,
Judge not your chosen plight.
Remember all is perfect,
Just sustain faith in the night.

All is but illusion,
The truth if it be told.
You are but a child in dream time,
So wake up and claim God's soul.

This dream we have been living,
It tells of such great plight,
Until we can remember,
And consciously reunite.

To reunite with God's love,
Is but to go home,
To our heavenly kingdom,
Where all sit upon their thrones.

Not thrones of greed or love's lust,
But thrones of God's true grace.
A grace that is a blessing.
The blessing based in faith.

Trust you shall awaken,
And find your rightful place,
Among the hosts of heaven,
That reside in God's embrace.

As we continue to weave this holographic timeless tapestry, I find myself remembering – as if it were this very moment – the most exciting spiritual experience so far in my journey. Even though it is difficult to pick just one event because there are so many, this one stands out.

I was all alone in my king size bed at the center in Shenandoah. Jon and Mike had stopped visiting me in the night. They were getting older and more secure in their surroundings. On this night there wasn't a cat or a dog to be found in my bedroom. I had just put my head on my pillow. As I looked to my left I saw a beautiful light being sitting on the bed beside me. My mind flashed back to the time I was visited by the stranger who appeared in my bed in St. Michaels. This was very different. It was more like the snowman who had visited me when I was just four years old. Now I was a completely different person having the experience. There was no fear, only the immense love that I felt emanating from this being. We communicated telepathically. He was aware of my every thought even before I was. And then, at the same time, I was also aware of his thoughts. As the shock of seeing him came into my mind his thoughts of changing form or leaving came to me also. I sensed that he was capable of taking on any form that made me comfortable. Knowing that I didn't want him to change or leave, I assured him that I was not afraid and communicated that I wanted him to remain and not change shape. How could I fear him when he was so beautiful? An intense feeling of deep love and security filled my whole being – the purest unconditional love – at a level I had never experienced.

He had large blue eyes which were slightly slanted. There was no clothing on his body which was almost not solid in form. The light around him was so bright it was difficult to look through the glow to see if there was a hard surface or skin as we have. His tiny nose was just above a small mouth, and his head was slightly larger at the top and back than ours.

I noticed that he had narrow shoulders and a thin neck with fluid arms, and hands much like mine, but his fingers seemed pointed at the tips. He was so graceful that when he moved it seemed as though he had no rigid skeletal structure. His gender was just something that I knew inside because he displayed no physical evidence that would make one think he was either male or female.

As I sat in his presence feeling his warm love, it occurred to me to ask for a healing. I had been attempting to rid my physical body of some uterine cysts so I assumed he would touch my stomach area. To my surprise, when I asked, he reached out his thin, fluid arm, and with the tip of his index finger, touched the side of my left breast. Even though it may sound odd, at first because of my confusion, I thought he was getting fresh with me. That thought quickly disappeared, as almost immediately after the touch, an intense wave of energy surged through every cell of my body. The energy seemed to come from around me. It entered through my back, and focused at my heart chakra, then left through the front of my body, after going through every other part of me. These indescribable, very intense waves of energy, kept coming in and going out creating a circular wave pattern that would rise and fall from my body. Although there was no sexual arousal, one could compare it to an orgasmic experience. But, even an orgasm would seem mild in comparison. Rapture is the only word that comes close to describing the feeling.

As the waves progressed, I was caught up in this wonderful feeling. My logical mind surfaced and when it did, so did fear. I was afraid that this beautiful being next to me would leave if I got too preoccupied with the experience. I made an effort to look in his direction and realized he was not where he had been. Then, almost in the same instant of the realization as I looked down at my body, I discovered that I was not there either. It was as though we had merged and became one energy light force. From that thought I lost my conscious memory and was taken into an altered dream-like state.

I can still remember every detail. In many ways it was more real than my everyday world. The light being and I were together in an empty schoolroom. We were very happy to be together once more. He came to me and when our hands joined, we became weightless and floated up in midair. Our bodies were fully extended behind us as if we were holding hands and lying on our stomachs in mid-air. Gazing lovingly in each other's eyes, we started to spin. We spun faster and faster until in a sudden burst of light our essences merged and became one. Now one radiant ball of blazing golden light, we bounced joyfully all around the room.

We then returned to our original form and holding hands, left the school and floated down the street. His thoughts and my thoughts were as one. We no longer had to walk; gravity wasn't as dense as it had been. We looked like the pictures of the angels that float just above the earth and lean forward slightly as they go forth. Everything seemed different. We saw cars standing still. All power was cut off. People were standing dazed in the middle of the road in total disbelief at what was happening. They had blank expressions on their faces and appeared to be in shock. Some sat quietly while others were in fear. All man-made things and power had come to a complete halt. All that remained was the true nature of creation, much like the way it seems here today as I write during this snow storm. There was also the feeling that linear time as we understand it no longer existed. The whole planet had come to a stop.

As we traveled down the road together, no one seemed to notice us. They were too caught up in their own stuff to care about seeing a light being and an ordinary woman floating down the street while holding hands. I remember thinking to him, "Isn't it wonderful that we can finally be together in public and openly have this relationship without fear of prejudice?" We had come out of the closet and were publicly announcing our love for each other. The dimensions had merged as our essence had merged in the schoolroom.

I saw this dream as a window to the future; a future when we would be as one again. My logical mind still has difficulty trying to explain just what happened that night, but I don't worry much about that any more. Explaining everything no longer seems important. The beauty of our brief moment together is etched in my memory and I am firm in my faith that it really did happen just as I have written.

Shortly after the visitation, I went to the doctor for a

mammogram. I had cysts in my right breast and was concerned that the lumps might be cancerous. To my surprise the mammogram showed a calcified lump in my left breast that I didn't know existed. It hadn't been there the year before. There was no explanation for this calcification and it was determined that it was not cancerous. I thought it was interesting that this calcification was in the exact same spot my visitor had chosen to touch when I asked for a healing.

The lines of communication with the other worlds seemed to open up even more after this experience. I was learning to trust my guidance with total faith, even though in that moment, it might not be clear why I was told to do things.

Back in the moment of writing, it has been a long day. I started writing at 5:30 a.m., when the electricity went off. One of my sons has just returned home from the ski resort. He is in bed now totally exhausted from two days of skiing. I am writing these words by flashlight because we still have no power.

Being alone and with no distractions, I was able to write all through the day. I discovered that the inner voices are always with me. They just get drowned out by the chaos we create for ourselves in our busy lives.

It is time to turn off the flashlight and drift into dream time, a whole book in itself. Who knows, maybe in my dreams I will find once more the light being who visited me.

Chapter 13

I received the message that it was time to move from Shenandoah – the Crystal Rainbow Center. The signs were very clear. Mohammed had sold his share of the cattle ranch to his cousin. Mohammed's cousin was not like our previous landlord. He was not willing to pay for any repairs or upkeep on either of the two houses or the property. The lawn was now our responsibility as was anything else that might go wrong. The farmer was no longer happy with the arrangement and took his cattle away. The final message came from nature when our water stopped flowing. I had been taught that this showed that there was a block in spirit flowing. Water was representative of spirit. Our new landlord refused to fix the problem and I knew it was a major one. He asked if I wished to purchase the house. It was old and because we lived in it, we knew all its many problems. With no water flowing the only answer was to move.

The house in St. Michaels had been on the market for over three years and still hadn't sold. We hadn't found any land for the center we thought we were to build and even if we had, without the sale of my house, we would not have the money to purchase it. Samuel had already moved in with our friend Orpha as he had more clients in the Washington, D.C. area. The logical choice seemed to be to move back to St. Michaels. The boys were in agreement.

They loved the idea of being with old friends and spending time with their Uncle Eddie who still lived there. We had visited but not that often and I knew that even though they liked Virginia, they would be happy to go back to their first home.

As for me it was bittersweet. I really had no desire to return. The thought of going back to the past was not my cup of tea. Just thinking about the past had always brought up unhappy memories or fears. I much preferred being in the moment and planning the future. So with that in my mind, I decided to go back in a different way – as a new person, living in the moment, and not connected to the past in the same way.

This was all I could do anyway. Our budget was very tight. If we moved elsewhere we would have to pay rent. My work, doing regressions, Reiki, and the workshops brought very little money into the family budget and the earnings from the sale of my self-published books almost covered the cost of the printing. I was now home schooling the boys. (The best decision we ever made.) There was very little time left after I finished writing, studying, giving workshops, and teaching Jon and Mike. God was my boss so the schedule always worked perfectly. Things were done in priority – when we got to them. Housework was at the bottom of the list, as it still is today.

We packed up and went back to St. Michaels. I had given up my three year search for land in Virginia. A little confused, I still had faith in my guidance and knew I was doing the best for my family. It may have appeared that we had been defeated because we didn't have a retreat center. Others would not know what we had learned. I wouldn't change one thread in the tapestry we had just woven together. I told the boys that home was wherever we were together and the healing center was in our hearts. Now we could be happy anywhere we went.

Jon and Mike enjoyed seeing their old friends and playing in the Miles River. They caught fish and crabs and gathered oysters in the shallow water. They were proud whenever they provided our meal. Their Uncle Ed, who had been like a second father to them, lived nearby. He would visit and take them out on his boat fishing. I have a picture of Jon holding up a blue fish that he caught that was almost as big as he was.

We were there for just a short time when the house sold. We were almost unpacked when it was time to pack again. The closing would be in just two months. Not much time but by now I had a lot of practice. Material things became a burden – something more to take care of. I decided to sell even more than I had before the first move from St. Michaels. All my antiques (things from the past) would be sold. We went from having three houses to care for to the prospect of no place to live. At least we would have money in our pockets and would be free to buy a new home when we found it. Where would we look? We didn't have a clue. Everything seemed to be happening so fast. We waited forever to sell the house and now that it was sold, it seemed too quick.

I decided to go within to find direction. While meditating one day, I saw the picture of a motor home. Even though I had never driven anything larger than a Volvo station wagon, I started looking for that motor home. It was found and purchased within one week. Now we were the proud owners of a thirty-five foot Cruise Air II, with power everything. It even had an electric sofa that opened to become a bed. The motor home slept as many as eight people comfortably. A tow-bar was purchased so the car could be pulled along behind us.

The purchase had been made in Annapolis and the Chesapeake Bay stood between the motor home and our garage. The thought of driving that huge vehicle across that very tall and long bridge scared the hell out of me. (Pardon my language, but that was exactly how I felt.) I had been in the moment, following inner guidance that had never steered me wrong. Now I was in the moment of having to drive this big thing. If there had been a God outside of me I would have cursed Him or Her for getting me into this. My way out of the moment was not to curse God, but to ask Ed to bail me out and give me some more time to get used to the idea of driving the motor home. He agreed to go with me to pick it up and drive it back to St. Michaels. Later he told me he hadn't realized how big it was and even he was a little intimidated by it.

There it sat in front of the garage. It took a couple of weeks before I got up the courage to drive it in a test run around the block. If I could drive it on the narrow back streets of St. Michaels, then I could go anywhere. I asked the boys, "Would you like to go for a ride around the neighborhood in the our new home?"

They gave each other that we know better than to do that look, and in unison said, "No." Then Jon said, "I'll stay here and watch. I'm not getting in that thing with you behind the wheel."

This didn't do much for my confidence. It was impossible to

change their minds so I went solo. They stood and watched as I pulled out of the driveway grateful that Ed had backed in so I could drive straight ahead and not have to back it up. Going forward was enough for me to handle.

As I sat in the overstuffed swivel seat, the realization of the spot I was in put an uneasy feeling in the pit of my stomach. The feeling subsided as I went within and remembered to have faith. This gave me the courage to go on. I must drive this thing whether I liked it or not. I would release my fears. The best way for me to do that was stay present in the moment. In this moment, I hadn't hit anything. In this moment, there had been no bad experience to be afraid of. So I turned the key, put my foot on the gas, took off the brake, and waved to my sons – who were wondering if they would ever see mom again. (Probably a slight over statement.) I surrendered my fear and was amazed at how easy it was to drive. Of course I picked a time of the day when few cars were on the road; at this point coping with traffic was out of the question.

I went out every day and practiced. The boys even decided that I looked like I knew what I was doing and agreed to go with me. They now seemed excited about our new home on wheels, and I was glad I had chosen this vehicle. We even went out on the highway and drove to the next town.

Everything had been sold or put in storage and we said a final goodbye to the house where the boys had been born and Pete had passed over to the other side. Bittersweet memories flooded over me as we drove out of town – the two boys, two dogs, three cats, and me.

We didn't have a clue where we would end up and that was exciting. I had faith that if we followed our inner guidance the journey would be perfect.

I was feeling quite accomplished with the ease in which I could handle this over forty-five foot vehicle. (When you add the car and tow bar to the thirty-five foot motor home you get about that length.) The boys were given specific duties. One would read the map and navigate, and figure mileage and times of arrival. The other was the lookout on my blind side. This kept me from hitting someone if I wanted to pass. The only way to see completely around the vehicle was to use mirrors and I was not accustomed to relying only on them. I was glad to have the boys to tell me what was on the road that I couldn't see.

About one hour into our virgin voyage, at the top and middle of the Chesapeake Bay Bridge, there was a very loud noise. I called to my lookouts, "Mike, Jon, what was that!"

They yelled back, "It was our awning. It ripped off." The thirty foot awning that we had carefully secured had been hit by a severe crosswind on the top span of the bridge and was now lying peacefully on the side of the road. It had bounced off a dump truck that was driving right next to us. I stayed in the moment and remained calm. I couldn't stop in the middle of the bridge so I would stop at the guard station on the other side of the tollbooths.

When we got to the other side, the dump truck driver pulled off and we got out and assessed any damages. The bridge police were there also. No damage was done to the truck or my motor home, but the awning was still out in the middle of the bridge. It wasn't blocking traffic but someone had to go and get it. They wanted me to take it but I didn't know what to do with it. Since it had been ripped off there was no way of attaching it again and it was too long to put inside. I told the officers if they went to get it they could have it to sell for scrap metal. They agreed and I drove off without my awning. I wasn't upset reasoning that no one had gotten hurt, the insurance would pay for a new awning, and I hadn't been to blame for anything. The trooper said that RVs lost awnings on the bridge to crosswinds all the time and I had been lucky. I knew luck had nothing to do with it.

All of this only amounted to a twenty minute delay in our trip. We had plans to meet Betty where she was living in Swannanoa, Virginia, and spend the weekend with her and her husband, Bruce. Betty was leading a meditation that night at the University of Science and Philosophy and I was invited. That weekend we were to meet another friend traveling in a motor home and together drive to Ashville North Carolina. A reunion of old friends and spiritual family had been planned for the following week and it was on the way to what I thought was my final destination, Florida.

My cousin, Anna, who lived on the Gulf Coast of Florida, offered to let us rent a house that she owned in Gainesville. We had visited Anna on a vacation the year before and liked the area so we decided to use this house as home base. We could travel in the motor home and check out the whole area for possible home sites. I sent her a check and asked her to have the power turned on so the house would be ready for us when we arrived.

The motor home provided us with a great deal of freedom. We could pick up at any moment and go where ever we were guided to go. Our travels would provide us with the opportunity to try living in many places. This would make our decision about where we were to live easier.

While learning to follow Spirit, I had learned that often the information we get at the soul level is on a need-to-know basis, much like when you work for the government. You are told in the moment only what you need to know to perform a specific task, or you are told what you want to hear so that you will go in a specific direction. The outcome isn't always what we think it will be. However all paths, even though they may not appear to, lead to the same place. We may not be aware of the true purpose or our final destination until we are there. There are also those occasions when we may never discover why we were guided in the way that we were. This understanding would come in handy on the journey we were embarking on.

I had just recovered from the incident with the awning – remember this was our first trip out of the neighborhood – when two miles from our destination, smoke started coming into the cabin. All power stopped. I managed to pull off the interstate and onto the shoulder of the highway. The boys and I grabbed the cats and dogs and before we could get out on the side of the road, a volunteer fireman in full dress stopped. He had been following us and saw the flames coming out from our engine. He quickly put out the fire with a fire extinguisher, preventing any further damage. Then two more volunteers from the fire department who were going home after putting out another fire, stopped in a pickup truck. They offered to take us anywhere we needed to go. A man wearing an expensive suit and driving a very impressive car also stopped to help us. He offered me the use of his phone. (At that time very few people had mobile phones.) I looked in his car and saw something interesting on the back seat. (A message from spirit.) This man was traveling around the country giving workshops. Inside his car were boxes of videos, all with the same title; "Claim Your Power, Claim Your Power..." What a message.

Using his phone I called Betty at Swannanoa, home of the University of Science and Philosophy. I explained what had happened and asked her if we could stay there for at least one night. We had planned to be sleeping in our new motor home, but it was being towed off the mountain as we spoke. Shirley, who was the director of the University at that time, told Betty it was all right for us to come. So we packed everyone up in the back of the pickup truck and left all our material possessions on the interstate.

When we arrived the meditation hadn't begun yet. I joined the group and told everyone the incredible story of what had happened that day. Then I found out that a stone cottage, which had been vacant, was just remodeled and suitable for us to stay in. The pets were no problem and everyone was eager to help us until we were out of this temporary predicament.

It was an adorable stone cottage with two bedrooms and a fully equipped kitchen. There were even linens, and fully made beds. Everything we needed was already there. The cottage was located in back of the Swannanoa Palace next to a meditation fountain and a real Persian Prayer tower. There was a great view of the formal gardens and a three-story Christ statue that had been made by Walter Russell. We were just close enough to be a part of everything but far enough away to have privacy. What was to be a short stay ended up being six and a half weeks. How that came to be, as Paul Harvey would say, is the rest of the story.

Chapter 14

While in my car driving into Charlottesville, which is just forty minutes from where we live in Glass Hollow, a little miracle happened. I was thinking, "This lifetime has been an incredibly magical journey." No sooner had that thought entered my mind when there in front of me, printed on the back of the next car, was the word "MAGIC" in very large black letters. I started crying and wondered, "Why the tears? Why am I having this emotional release?"

Every time Spirit, Universal Consciousness, God (whatever name you may choose) talks to me the joy of the truth fills my heart. I teach that we are not alone – that we are not separate. What the teacher is teaching is what that teacher has come to learn through their personal life experience. This Universal Law, without exception is true. We are what we teach because we have learned through that experience.

You might take note of different groups, individuals or religions. Ask yourself what do they teach? What is their message based on? Then notice the people around them that have come to learn and live those messages. You may find that many of the people that are drawn to be there are learning those lessons or in some manner teaching them.

An example might be a place that teaches Universal Love

and Oneness. When you live there, you notice that all of the people are at some level learning to open their hearts and remember that they are one with the Universe – God. Because they have not found this and are still seeking it, they will be anything but loving, at peace, or in the union of the oneness. This brings us to the rest of the story.

Getting back to Swannanoa – after the fire in the motor home there was so much to be grateful for. The insurance company paid for our food and lodging until our motor home was repaired. Since we hadn't owned the vehicle for more than thirty days, the dealership where it was purchased was responsible for parts and labor to fix it. None of our personal possessions were damaged. Most important of all, no one was injured. We had a wonderful place to stay and good friends to be with.

Believing as I do that there are no mistakes or accidents and everything has a purpose, I asked Spirit, "Why have we been stopped on Afton Mountain and brought to Swannanoa? It is clear that we are being taken care of. We even have an extra one thousand dollars for the awning that blew off on the Bay Bridge. But what is the deeper meaning of it all?"

The answer from Spirit was, "*Live in the moment. Don't get caught up in the past or future plans. Make as few plans or time tables as possible. Plan only for the day and moment you are in.*"

Armed with this message, I called the garage and was informed, "Your transmission overheated and set off the fire. You will have to wait for a new one to be shipped. We will be lucky if we can find one. We will let you know how long it will be." While we waited for the parts to be found, shipped, and installed, we started our journey of living in the moment and following the guidance of Spirit – the Universal One – God. There were no appointments, no 9 to 5 job, no responsibilities of housekeeping, the house being in the repair shop. This was a vacation from the world – a world we had until then lived in.

One day in meditation, Spirit reminded me of a message that had been given to me before we left St. Michaels, *"Tell Bruce and Betty they are to leave the Palace at Swannanoa and go with you to Florida."* This reminded me of the first time I got a message for Betty and was reluctant to give it to her because it sounded so absurd. Much had happened since our first meeting and there was no doubt this time what I must do.

Bruce answered the phone at the Palace, "We are really happy here. I am caretaker of the gardens and I love my job."

This didn't make it easier to deliver the message. I was reluctant to tell him knowing how he would probably react. I waited until Bruce was off the phone and gave the message to Betty. She, on the other hand, would at least consult her guidance before rejecting the offer. "Betty sit down I've got a message for you from Spirit. You and Bruce are to leave the Palace and go with me and the boys to Florida. I know you probably don't want to hear this but all the same it was my guidance to call and deliver the message. You can do with it what you choose. We are planning to stop at Swannanoa on our way to North Carolina and then Florida. My cousin owns a house we can use as home base while we go out in the motor home to find land or a place to live permanently. You and

Bruce are welcome to come with us to explore new territories and possibilities."

Betty was very quiet on the other end of the phone. Then she said, "I'll have to ask Spirit." She turned to Bruce and told him my offer.

Bruce got back on the phone. "Thanks for the offer but I'm not leaving here." For the moment, at least in Bruce's mind, the subject was closed. He had made his decision. Because he was so adamant about staying, we all just forgot about the message.

I was offering this suggestion to them only because I had been guided to. Personally I wasn't looking forward to the prospect of all of us traveling and living in such small quarters. It would be difficult enough fitting all our things in the motor home. The idea of adding their belongings to the equation didn't add up. Nevertheless, if Spirit wanted us to do it there must be a good reason. When we got to Florida, we could unload all the extra stuff at the house so we could manage for a short period of time in those close quarters. Then maybe Bruce and Betty would enjoy staying at the house while the boys and I went out exploring.

I released any attachment to whatever the outcome might be and turned it all over to the Universal One – knowing that whatever might happen, it would be in the highest good for all. It had always been so in the past when I followed Spirit.

The focus now was on spiritual work. Spirit started sending people to me. They would just show up in the garden or at the front door of the stone cottage and I would be guided as to what to say or do.

Patricia, a friend who was also living in the Palace of Swannanoa, paid me a visit. In the past we had worked well together. She is a channel and has the gift of speaking in tongues, which I call the language of the angels or the language of light. Sometimes I would lead a meditation or channel and she would interpret it in what she called the language of the angels. My voice was echoed by the voices of the angels. This always gave me a special feeling, magnifying and enhancing whatever came through.

We went to work to pay the university back for allowing us to stay there by doing healing on the grounds. We worked together, discovering old scars and wounds that had been stored energetically on the land for many years; talking to the spirit of Afton Mountain and those that had lived there and passed to the other side.

The University of Science and Philosophy, established by Walter and Lao Russell, leased the palace of Swannanoa. The palace is located on Afton Mountain at the beginning of the Blue Ridge Parkway.

We discovered that Afton Mountain, one of the oldest in the world, draws people to be healed, assisting them in opening their hearts and releasing their fears and anger. Some say Swannanoa is at the center of a huge vortex of heart centered and clearing energy. Because these stored energies are invisible to the human eye they could lie silently like undesired litter without notice. Patricia and I were just picking up emotional litter and releasing it from the vortex which held it in place within a spiral field of energy. Our prayer was that it be transmuted for the highest good of all to the highest vibration of love and light. By recycling the energies that were there the vortex was enhanced. Because Patricia and I were both empathic, we could feel the anger or sadness as we walked through these energy spirals. That's just what we did. We walked and talked to the earth and rocks. We prayed and we felt great love and a long overdue clearing of old emotional energies.

Weeks passed and still the transmission for the motor home had not arrived. Everyone at the University of Science and Philosophy was getting ready for what was called *Homecoming*. Once every year, alumni and friends would gather for a long weekend celebration. There were speakers, workshops, fun, and reunions of the heart. Tension was mounting in the staff as the time of this event grew nearer. The boys and I had offered our services. Mike and Jon helped Bruce in the gardens and so did Betty and I. We all pitched in and did whatever was needed.

Most of my time went to peace making. People were not getting along and that included Bruce and Betty. I found myself learning how to stay in Christ Consciousness – being the neutral observer or mediator, and maintaining a space of unconditional love and acceptance for both sides of every issue. A wonderful opportunity for spiritual growth was created as a result of this situation. As is often the case, this doesn't necessarily mean I enjoyed the experience. It did, however, show me how much there was to learn about maintaining this state of consciousness in stressful situations.

Many times the children can teach us the most. When riding to town one day, Bruce and Betty were having another argument. They were in the back seat with Mikie. Jon and I were in the front seat. Stopping the argument, Bruce asked, "Master Mike, do you have any spiritual advice for me? How can I get along better with Betty?"

Mike said, "Sure, but it will cost you a penny a minute." Bruce agreed to the arrangement. Mike thought for just a minute and then said, "Just love her no matter what."

Not to agree with one side or the other sometimes felt like a risk. My friends wanted me to be loyal to them. When I couldn't because it would mean taking sides, I risked losing their friendship because they felt betrayed. Just listening and not passing any judgment seemed to work the best. When no one feels judged they are less likely to attack or feel they have to defend their position. The struggle soon disappears and the truth that we are all one and there is nothing to judge is more easily felt and remembered. So I followed my son's advice to Bruce and just loved everyone no matter what.

As I looked around, it occurred to me that everyone including myself had come to the mountain to learn unconditional love and acceptance. We weren't just learning this from a book, we were learning to live it – walking our talk. This is what Walter and Lao Russell had stressed in their teachings at the University. This was what everyone who went to Swannanoa had come to learn – unconditional love and universal oneness. With all that was going on around me I found the perfect opportunity to learn and live the principles they taught. My job was now to listen to both sides of every issue and stay out of judgment. Judgment creates separation and the idea was to unify – seeing through the eyes of the soul.

During this time, I was also looking for property for a group from the Light Center in Washington, where in the past I had done workshops. This group wanted to create a retreat center in the mountains. Cheryl, a real estate agent Betty told me about, was showing me large estates with hundreds of acres – out of my price range. I had given up looking for land in the area for myself. Cheryl called to tell me about a piece of land that was for sale by a private owner, "Joyce, you must go to look at this land. I don't stand to make anything from the sale. The owner won't even talk to me. My guidance is that this is your land." Cheryl also had learned to listen to spirit. This would be one of those times that I was glad she had.

I wasn't at all interested. It was only eighteen and a half acres and I wasn't looking for land of that size. I was going to Florida but Cheryl insisted that I just go and look. The strong guidance she was getting was similar to what I had gotten for others. So I listened. After all, she would receive no commission because this was a private sale. She had nothing to gain personally if I bought this property. I had plenty of extra time with my new-found freedom, and I was learning to be in the moment and listen to Spirit. Maybe this was Spirit's way of speaking to me – through another person.

I went to see the land. As I stood in the midst of the towering popular trees at the heart of the property, I fell in love. What a healing and peaceful place. It was completely isolated – in a hollow surrounded by mountains and on a circular ridge. I stood there knowing this was to be mine.

The price was right, just forty thousand dollars. The road

had already been cut in and a spot for the house and septic field cleared. The owner had planned to build an eight-sided log home there, but his wife had to have hip surgery and wanted to move to a warmer climate – Florida of all places. Imagine that.

After the sale of my house I had a lot of money waiting to be re-circulated. Why not invest in this property? I bought the lot on the spot. And have never regretted the decision. The next day after signing the papers I stopped in to see Rick. He had been showing me property in Nelson County for three and a half years but without success. He congratulated me on the purchase, and said he knew of someone who would buy it from me for fifty thousand dollars. As I saw it, the Universe had just given me a pay check for ten thousand dollars. I didn't sell – wise decision.

The third transmission was being installed in the motor home by this time. The first one was cracked in shipping. The second one was found to be faulty after they installed it. Three being a charm, we had hopes that this one would work. It just so happened that the timing was perfect as the Universe was revealing the reason for our long overdue departure.

Homecoming was over. Things were getting back to normal at the university; I had found the land; surely after six weeks we could go – right? I went to pick up our home. We were almost to Swannanoa, when in Waynesboro, just in front of the fire department, all power stopped again and we were halted once more.

As I went to get help inside the fire house I noticed on the wall pictures of a motor home that had burned down to the frame. You could still tell what make and model it was. I couldn't believe my eyes. It had been a Cruise Air II – just like ours. My frustration shifted to gratitude when I thought of what might have been our fate. The firemen told me of how often this occurred as people tried to get over the mountain. Many were not as blessed as we had been. I was now content to be patient and go back to the little stone cottage in Swannanoa to await further orders from Spirit.

It was getting a little awkward to say the least. Shirley, the director of the university had been a most gracious hostess. Every time a new transmission would go into the motor home, I would assure her we would soon be moving on. And each time something would happen to keep us from going. I was embarrassed having to go to see her again – feeling a bit like Calamity Jane.

Shirley was having problems of her own. She and Betty, who had been the best of friends, were on the outs. A huge fight ensued and Betty was fired. This was extremely unusual as Shirley had never fired anyone. She had a gift for keeping the peace and honoring everyone's wishes, which wasn't easy living in a heart chakra vortex like Swannanoa. Betty apparently had pushed one of her buttons on a bad day.

This was interesting because Betty wasn't even on the payroll. She had volunteered her services but managed to get fired anyway. Bruce was the only one of the two who received a paycheck and he spent most of his earnings buying flowers for the gardens. It didn't seem possible that this had happened.

I continued to play the role of peacemaker, not taking sides even though Betty was my close friend. I tried in vain to patch things up. Then the final piece of the puzzle became clear. The one thread of the tapestry that had not been woven yet. My mind flashed back to the guidance I had gotten months ago in St. Michaels. The guidance came from the future and that was why it didn't make any sense at the moment. Now it was perfectly clear and so was everything else. Bruce and Betty would go with us to Florida.

The next day the motor home was fixed for the last time and we were now really free to go. We all left together; Bruce, Betty, Mike, Jon, me, three cats and two dogs. Look out Florida here we come!

Releasing much fear, I got behind the wheel once more. Thoughts of our maiden voyage, the awning, and the fire hung in the back of my mind. I focused instead on the magic in the moment, and how everything that had happened had turned out for the best. We were soon having a great deal of fun setting out on a new adventure, living in the moment, and following what seemed to be the yellow brick road.

The motor home, though large, was a bit crammed now that we had two more people and all their possessions as well. The kitchen area was full of boxes. I gave Bruce and Betty my private bedroom with the queen-size bed. Mike and I would sleep on the electric sofa, which was quite comfortable. Jon slept in the pull-down bunk above the driver's seat at the front. The cats stayed in their carriers in the bathroom, and the dogs, Star and Mindy could sleep on the floor. Somehow it would work, but we were all looking forward to Florida and a little more leg room once we got to my cousin's house.

Two days later and in the middle of the night we arrived in Gainesville, Florida. It was very late so we decided to wait to explore our new surroundings. In the morning we were shocked to find that someone had vandalized the house. There was no electricity or water, even though I had sent plenty of money well in advance of our arrival. The pipes were torn out and so were some of the walls. Fire ants inhabited the front yard which made it difficult just to get out of the motor home – welcome to Florida!

The cats were getting tired of being cooped up so I put them in the larger bathroom of the house with food and a litter box, just until we figured out what to do next. It was obvious we could not live in this house. The fire ants seemed to seal the message that we were to leave. But where were we supposed to go? None of us had the answer.

We got in the car and just drove. I asked for guidance. Just two miles from the house we found a resort for motor homes – Beaver Springs. The decision was unanimous we would go on vacation and then figure out what to do next.

It was a great place. We spent our time outside and in the large club house with a giant fireplace. The boys swam and found many activities at the campground to keep them busy, and there was even food if we didn't want to cook. We got a few things repaired on the motor home that we discovered on the drive from Virginia, got more accustomed to each other living in such close quarters, and relaxed. The focus was on the positive, the adventure, and having the most fun we could in the moment. This was important after all the stresses and disappointments we had encountered. We soon forgot about the house and the fire ants. This had merely been a strong message from Spirit not to stay in Florida.

A few hours after finding the resort, we returned to the house in the car to get the cats. When I opened the door to the bathroom, Charity, our latest addition to the family, jumped out in fright, attacked Jon – who was just standing there, and bit him on the arm. Jon found Charity when we lived in Shenandoah and she had been his cat. She had her rabies shots so I wasn't too concerned about Jon but she was another story. Something had torn the skin off her back and she was bleeding. It didn't appear to be too serious a wound but we couldn't catch her. She seemed to disappear. After hours of searching we gave up and took Lady and Moon Beam, the other two cats, back to the resort.

Time and again we went to look for her and never found her. Two weeks passed and we had given up hope. The day before we were to leave I got the message to try once more. I drove up to that awful house and this time, there she was, sitting quietly in the front yard. Much more docile and feeling brave enough to venture out, she had come out from under the house where she must have hidden after her ordeal. However, we would discover that this was not the Charity that we had known and loved and she would never be quite the same again.

Charity never got over her fright. Her wound had almost healed itself but the emotional scars were lasting. The other animals sensed it too and did not want to accept her back into the family. She was now considered a stranger by the other animals and we learned we could no longer trust her. She had been so traumatized that she was biting and attacking everyone. It was clear we would have to let her go for the sake of everyone else in the group. This was a difficult decision for Jon who had loved her most but eventually he would agree to it.

As we left the resort we still didn't know where we were going. We only knew we couldn't stay there. Everyone had a vote as to which direction we would go. Some said the Keys. That sounded good. So we headed south. Then on the radio, the news of snipers shooting at tourists in their cars, gave us a clear message not to go in that direction. Bruce and Betty had met in Hawaii and Bruce had originally been from Southern California. Maybe we should go west. In any event, we had all had enough of Sunny Florida. We decided to go to the West Coast.

Driving along the gulf coast to Gulf Breeze, we stayed at the home of the Blue Angels – on a naval base. Because my husband Pete had been retired from the Navy, we qualified to stay at the motor courts on base. This had many advantages. It was safe, affordable, and I could shop at the commissary and base post exchange. They also had a veterinarian. I took Charity to the vet and released her. Her wound was completely healed now but the vet stilled checked her. She was very helpful and agreed to try to find a home for her but admitted it might be difficult but she would do her best. We all prayed that she would find a better home because it was clear she wasn't happy living in the motor home with all of us.

We left the base and the next day we were in Texas and staying in a campground located in a pecan grove. Lady and Moon Beam, the other two cats, escaped one night when Bruce was leaving the motor home. He had a habit of moving slowly and leaving the door open. Since we now let the cats roam the motor home, they took this opportunity to sneak out. The next morning Lady was the only one to return.

When I opened the door that morning to go out, a wide-eyed Lady flew past me and hid under the kitchen table in between some boxes. She was covered with black grease. She would never be tempted to go out again. One of the permanent residents of the motor court told us that coyotes must have gotten Moon Beam. Until then, wild animals had not been in the picture. Lady, being a survivor, had hidden all night up in the motor of our vehicle. We never found Moon Beam and this broke my heart as she was my favorite of the three cats and had been Lady's daughter. She and Star, our black lab, were best buddies and I know Star missed her most.

We were now down to two dogs and one cat. But that wasn't the end of the exodus. Mindy, who was now fifteen, almost blind, and deaf, was having trouble getting in and out of the motor home. Her legs were very short and because of her bad hips she had difficulty going up and down the steep steps. I was the only one she would allow to pick her up because she was in so much pain.

Before I took her in, Mindy had two hip surgeries, which meant that there was nothing further that could be done to mend her hips. Her previous owners couldn't keep her. I heard about her and knew she would be hard to place in a home so I took her. She was a one person dog. She never got along well with anyone but me, and I was quite attached to her. Mindy reminded me a great deal of my husband's dog and close companion, Midnight. They had the same type of personality and I imagined that perhaps Pete had sent Mindy from the other side to keep me company. Time after time I watched her fall on her head as she attempted to come in and go out. It had gotten so bad Mindy wouldn't even allow me to pick her up. Obviously she was in severe pain. Her appetite was gone and she was wasting away. She had also developed a terrible odor. From past experience with other dogs, I knew she didn't have long to live. Under normal conditions I would have allowed her to peacefully slip away – letting nature take its course. Living as we were this was not an option.

As we pulled off the interstate somewhere in Texas, I made a decision. On the off ramp just in front of the campground we had chosen to stay in, there was a big sign – Veterinarian. It was best to act fast – in the moment – so that afternoon, with tears in my eyes, I took Mindy to the other side. It was one of the hardest things I've ever done, and so soon after saying goodbye to Charity and Moon Beam.

This was much more difficult. *I* must be the one to take her as she trusted me. The vet was most compassionate. He assured me that I was doing the best thing for her because she was in so much pain and nothing could be done to help her. I talked to her and said my good-byes. I know she thanks me for what I did. As I write about this the tears have come up again. It is almost as if I just said good-bye to her once more.

Now we were traveling with only one cat, Lady and one dog, Star. In just one week we had lost three very loved members of our family. This was definitely the lowest point of the trip.

To lift our spirits we looked to the future and our adventure. Indiana Jones was popular with all of us, so we watched all three of his movies. Bruce started to wear his Indiana Jones hat and we kidded around about going to look for lost treasure or maybe even gold. Then one day Bruce told us a secret, "I own a real gold mine in California. I mined it for several years with a friend who passed away. I am now sole owner of the dig. We never found the mother lode but we did find some gold." Bruce had spent years prospecting. He and his friend were looking for Peg Leg Smith's lost gold mine. This mine is a legend in the Borrego desert in Southern California where he property was located. Bruce told us about Peg Leg and then said, "I never found much but I 'm sure it's there somewhere."

This was something the boys could get excited about – hidden treasure – gold. We all got a little gold fever, especially Betty, who until that moment didn't know her new husband owned a gold mine.

We had a lot of fun watching Indiana Jones and planning the future digs. This was just the medicine we needed to bind us closer together as a family with a common goal – gold. Focusing on the moment, all our moods shifted, and we were having fun once more.

Along the way to California, we stopped at the state parks to camp and took advantage of the free educational services each state offered. We had a computer set up so the boys could do their studies. Geography was top of the list of courses. They learned firsthand where all the southern states were and what they were like. They became experts at navigation and hitching up the car to a tow bar. One man in a camp ground where we stayed taught auto mechanics to Jon. He showed him how to grease the motor home and change the oil which boosted Jon's self-esteem. That was important especially for a thirteen year-old boy without a father.

We had reached Southern California, a wide open and truly beautiful state. The desert was no exception. I had never been in a desert environment and neither had Jon and Mike. It was winter, apparently the best time of the year to be there. The park rangers taught classes on all the things we were interested in. We went to lectures about mastodon bones that had been found at a nearby archaeological site, looked at the stars through special telescopes, and went out to different locations to see fault lines that were actively moving as a result of earthquakes. As we stood on these sites, we could sometimes feel the shaking of the ground under our feet and hear the rumbling echo that it would create in the nearby mountains. There were cave drawing and archaeological sites where native people once lived. We saw evidence that the whole desert had once been a lush green mesa – vastly different from the present. Mike and Jon were able to interact on these tours and lectures with the adults. I was impressed with their ability to participate without feeling intimidated as they learned and contributed to the group with their own insights and questions. Every minute seemed special – magical.

A jeep was rented so we could go to the gold mine. Before we went to the site, as a matter of respect for Peg Leg Smith and to pay homage to his legend, we visited a big pile of rocks. Sure enough, there in the desert was a mail box; in it was a book to sign, if you were going to look for the lost mine. You were to sign the book, pick out a rock from the surrounding area, and deposit it on the pile. Apparently we weren't the only ones to know about the lost gold mine. But *we* would be successful.

Bruce's property was way off the road. It took hours to get to it every day as the road soon disappeared and despite the jeep, we had to go in on foot the rest of the way. We saw a herd of long-horned sheep and were told that this was rare so we felt especially blessed. The experience was so exciting that even if we found no gold, it was well worth the effort.

Bruce and Betty asked if I would channel information hoping it would help in the search for the mine. I sat on one of the large boulders, took a few deep breaths and said, *"The gold is in your heart. You are the gold. The gold is the truth. When you find the truth you will have found the gold."*

This was not what everyone wanted to hear. They wanted instructions as to where to dig or what landmark to look for. The fact that we already possessed what we were looking for wouldn't fill our pockets with money. And then it happened. Jon had gone with Mike and Bruce up the side of the mountain to a spot that Bruce had mined in the past. As they were coming back down, Jon slipped and fell, sliding about ten feet. He didn't hurt himself but when he stood up he had a rock in his hand. He went to Bruce and said, "Is this what it looks like."

"Yes! That's it. That's gold." Bruce said. Jon had come up with the only physical gold we would find – a nice sized rock that we still have. Bruce said, "That's more gold than I found in three years." Sadly, the mother lode eluded us and it was time to take back the jeep I had rented. We focused on finding the gold in our hearts.

Later at our nearby campsite, Jon fell off his bike. He came running back to the motor home. I thought he had hurt himself but instead, he had another rock in his hand. He had struck gold again. We teased him, "Hey Jon, why don't you go and fall again and bring home some more gold?"

We camped at Clark's Dry Lake often and found out later from some of the local residents that it might have been a listening station. Large satellite dishes had been set up in various locations around the lake and near a house, which was surrounded by a tall barbed wire fence. The station was abandoned and the dishes removed. The reason given was lack of funding. As rumor had it, signals had been sent out in an attempt to make contact with life in the cosmos. They would listen in hopes of hearing some messages coming back from intelligent life on another planet. At least that was the local gossip.

We heard from others that people came from all over the world to have ET experiences at Clark's Dry Lake. It was a very remote camping area. On weekdays, the only other occupants of that part of the desert were coyotes. We would gather wood for a campfire. When it got dark we would all sit around it, except for Lady who still hadn't come out of the motor home after what happened in Texas. Then we would go inside and play canasta, a card game Bruce taught us, by candlelight – no electricity. This was a very special time living on our own, away from civilization. At the end of the day we would blow out the candles and turn in.

The only light now was the moon, if it was out, and the stars that looked like they had been painted in the sky. They appeared so close, one almost felt they were in one's lap, or by just reaching out one may touch them. There was a silence that could not be found elsewhere. With the exception of the occasional rumbling of the earth, or Star's conversations with the coyotes when they got near our campsite, there was only silence.

It was on one of these very dark and very silent nights, as I lay looking out at the stars through the window, that I saw one of the lights on the horizon of the distant mountains move. As it got closer, I noticed it was made up of two elliptical rings of lights. The ring on the bottom was smaller than the ring just above it. In the past, I had seen light vehicles on the ceiling in Shenandoah. That was during my many out-of-body experiences as I now explained them. This light looked different, for as it went over the motor home, it disappeared. I now knew this wasn't an out-of–body experience. It wasn't the kind of vehicle that my astral body had traveled in. This was a real nuts-and-bolts vessel in the third dimension. Looking out the opposite window, I watched for it to appear on the other side of the motor home, but saw nothing. Instead, I heard something land on top of us. There was a loud thud and the whole vehicle started to move back and forth. Whatever, or whoever had landed on top of us walked on two feet down the length of the motor home, then jumped off. I heard two feet land heavily in the sand outside the window.

I yelled to the back, "Bruce did you hear that?"

"I sure did," he said.

I told everyone what I heard and they looked out the windows too. We all looked but it was too dark. We couldn't see anything. There were no trees or hills. The campsite was completely flat and open for miles. There weren't any large animals that could jump that high or walked on two feet. We never found an explanation for what had happened, and this was not the last strange thing to happen at this site.

Once a week we would go into town and camp at the national park. We could take showers. In the desert with no humidity, there wasn't the need for daily showers in winter. The boys could watch videos which we would rent and we could hike into the beautiful palm oasis just inside the park. I loved to watch the roadrunners (real birds, not just cartoons) as they quickly darted from place to place.

After a couple days of civilization the boys were ready to get back to the freedom they felt when we were on the dry lake. They had come full circle. In the beginning, they wanted to stay only in the resort-type campsites as even the state park wasn't good enough. They wanted cable TV, pool, and spas. Now they preferred nature; where there were no rules and regulations or complaining people when they ran or made noise. They had chosen well without my saying anything.

We usually had the dry lake all to ourselves. When an occasional camper would move in, it felt like an intrusion. We spent so much time there all by ourselves that sometimes it felt as though we were the only people on the planet. "Who were these strangers and how dare they interlope in our private world?"

As I lay in the complete silence, I began to hear unusual sounds – like nothing I had ever heard before. I noticed I only heard them when everything was very quiet. One night I asked the others if they heard it. When the sounds were called to their attention Mike and Betty also heard these beautiful harmonics – music of the spheres. The music almost sounded like the pipe organ in the movie *Close Encounters of the Third Kind*. I had been thinking about that movie a lot after the experience we had just had. For some reason, Jon and Bruce said they didn't hear anything. We wondered why some of us could clearly hear the tones and others could hear nothing.

This happened every night that we camped on the dry lake only when we were alone in the desert. I became obsessed with finding the source of the music – some logical explanation. One night I decided to go out and drive around the lake to investigate if the sounds might be coming from the house that was surrounded by the tall barbed wire fence; the one that was supposed to have been abandoned but was visited by moving vans and helicopters regularly. We noticed a lot of activity at this *abandoned* site.

Jon didn't want me to go by myself and I couldn't convince anyone else to go with me, but I was determined to go, and I did. I got in the car and drove up to the area in question. The car doors were locked and the window was down just enough to listen. I turned off the car and just sat quietly listening to the silence. That's all I heard – silence. I didn't stay long because I knew Jon would worry about me and since he only had one parent I'd better get back. I stopped on the way back at some of the places where the listening dishes had been dismantled. (Metal poles and cement bases still jutted out of the ground.) Again I would turn off the key and listen. It wasn't until I got closer to our vehicle that I could hear anything. Then I noticed that the closer I got to home the clearer I could hear the sounds – the harmonics. When I went inside the motor home, the sound was the loudest. How could this be? Was this music being made by our vehicle? We didn't even use the generator. Why didn't we hear it when we camped elsewhere?

I was more puzzled than ever. This wasn't what I had expected. Then I noticed if I went to the back of the RV it wasn't as loud. It seemed louder in one particular part of the motor home; directly under, guess what, our large antenna that was mounted on the roof. Were we receiving the music of the spheres? Had our vehicle become a listening device for the stars? We never established the source of the music but it was exciting thinking that it could have been from another galaxy somewhere, and we had the opportunity to actually hear it.

Chapter 15

Christmas was coming, but in the desert it didn't feel like it, so we drove about an hour up into the mountains to the Palomar Observatory to have a snowball fight. I was somehow able to avoid being hit. Betty however, who feared this possibility, of course got the worst of it. (What one fears is what one will often attract.) It was on this trip that I was guided to give everyone a special Christmas present. We would all go to Disneyland and Knotts Berry Farm. Bruce loved the idea; he was still a child at heart and these were his favorite places. The boys were also excited about the prospect. Since these weren't Betty's favorite spots, I had a special gift planned for her. I had been thinking about it for several months.

While we were still in Florida my guidance had been that when we got to California, I would gift Bruce and Betty with the air fare to Hawaii. Christmas seemed the perfect time to tell them what I had been guided to do. Since we were talking about Disneyland, I was starting to wonder how I would be able to afford both gifts. Not wanting to give in to lack consciousness, I pushed the fear of not having enough money to the side. In the moment there was no lack. I said my prayer, "Goodness to all concerned, and only Thy will being done, thank you Creator for sending us whatever is necessary to create the highest good for all." I turned it over to Spirit and told Bruce and Betty about their trip to Hawaii. They were happy about the idea since it had been their desire to go.

That same day on the way back to the desert some unbelievable guidance came through. We were *all* to go to Hawaii. How could that be? I barely had enough to pay for my friends. How could I also afford to pay for myself, and the two boys, plus all the extra expenses once we got to Hawaii? When I told everyone what Spirit had communicated there was a celebration in the car. Then everyone was praying – with goodness to all concerned of course.

Betty, who yearned to be back on the island where she had met her husband, went to work and things were starting to come together. She made a phone call to one of their friends whom they had stayed with before. She found out her friend was in India with her husband. Another friend Rebecca, was house sitting for them while they were in India. Rebecca was moving out the next week and a new house sitter was needed. Rebecca would contact the couple in India and get permission for all of us to stay for free in their condo. We called back in two days and received great news – permission was given and we now had a free place to stay. It was a place in which we could also cook our own meals – another savings.

If it was in our highest good to go, we knew things must flow. Otherwise, we would be creating out of our personal will which may not be in our best interest. (Have you ever wanted something and then wished you hadn't gotten it later?) We were learning that it is always better not to be attached to the outcome. That meant staying in the moment with complete faith that Spirit would take care of the details. Our job was just to go with the flow, in the moment, and allow the creation to unfold without fear of lack, limitation, or interference.

Other issues would have to be addressed. How does one get a motor home across the ocean? We joked about putting pontoons around it and paddling to Hawaii. That didn't seem too practical so a secure place to store it was found. Then there was the air fare for three adults and two children. Because we were leaving in mid-January, there were special rates available. Bruce and Betty would only need one-way fares because they planned to stay on the island. It was amazing how reasonable the rates were; even the boys qualified for a half-price fare with one accompanying adult.

Star and Lady were to go on vacation too. There was a resort for pets called the Desert Dog. It had extra-large, natural, outdoor enclosures and they could socialize with new friends. The cost there was also reduced because it was just after the holiday and they were looking for new clients.

A special deal was offered by a motel near the Los Angeles airport. If we paid for the night, we would be taken in the morning to the airport and our car would be stored in their underground garage at no cost. This also provided a place to stay when we returned to pick up the car. We had planned to be gone for at least four weeks and parking at the airport would have been twice what the room would cost. Plus we had free valet and shuttle service. There was a drive of several hours to get to Los Angeles. It would be easy to find the motel which was just off the freeway and it meant less stress for me. I didn't enjoy driving in city traffic in new territory.

With all the details taken care of, the way was clear for all of us to go to the island of Kauai, the garden isle – paradise. After a short stay in Disneyland where we all had a lot of fun we returned to the desert and prepared for a real adventure.

Things were going like clockwork. It was easy to find the motel and the next morning we were taken to the Los Angeles Airport. We had a great flight, and as the plane landed, the beauty I saw was impressive. What a change from the desert and Los Angeles! We rented a car and drove off to Princeville where the condo was located. The next day we heard that a strong earthquake had closed the LA airport just after we left. I wondered about my car in the underground garage. The car was insured so that fear was easy to let go of. Then we heard all the freeways were closed. I had to trust that all was in divine order. There was a whole month before we would return and there was nothing I could do to change things anyway. Spirit would take care of the details. This became my mantra.

Princeville lived up to its name – fit for royalty. A huge sculpted fountain of Neptune, king of the seas, greeted us at the entrance. We drove through the golf course to get to the condo which was a short distance from the ocean. The waves could be heard crashing on the shore as we walked past the pool to the door of our new residence. A flier for the Flower of Life Workshop was taped to the door. Rebecca, who had been staying at the condo left it for us. She was a facilitator and was giving the workshop for Drunvalo Melchizedek. At the time we weren't at all interested in the flier. Sacred geometry seemed too left-brained for me. Betty and I found a meditation tape from the workshop and we listened to it. We weren't impressed, so we went sightseeing and forgot about it. (We weren't listening to Spirit.)

The island was healing and we all found great peace just by being there. Our free tour guides, Bruce and Betty, were fantastic. Getting a resident's perspective and not the usual tourist treatment was something I always preferred. While in college I spent the summer in Ocean City, Maryland and because of that experience I had no desire to be a tourist. I was a waitress that summer and learned what it was like to be on the service side of a resort. Blending in and learning about the culture and the people was of more importance to me. It was easy to understand why the native people would resent the tourists. They relied on them for revenue but felt they had been invaded. What they had given up, peace, natural beauty, ancient culture, and autonomy, was priceless.

There were street markets where we shopped for food twice a week. They were held once a week on either side of the island. Local fruits and vegetables were available and sold by the residents. The prices were much better than in the traditional stores. Everything on the island had to be shipped in and this was costly. For local residents on lower budgets than the tourist, this was restrictive. Much of what was available to the tourist was not affordable for the native-born or local resident. It was possible to get a more intimate view of life on the island when trading with the growers.

Then there was the rich taste of the food – like nothing I had ever had before. Just a simple banana became a whole meal and tasted nothing like the bananas on the mainland. Many of our meals were just fruit or large salads. Of course the boys had to have their pizza, so we ate out on occasion too. There was so much to see and do that food played a less important role even though it was delicious and healthy.

Of course, the other dimensions were here too, and at night on the ceiling, my astral vision was turned on. On this island it was much easier to see beyond the physical world. I would focus my vision in a different way and stare, as one might meditate on a candle flame, looking deeper and deeper into the darkness. Almost every night, while looking at the ceiling, I was treated to views of the reefs and underwater scenes. Not being fond of swimming, I was happier seeing the surrounding ocean in this way. I could swim unencumbered, with the fish and even on occasion, dolphins, while I lay in bed.

We had been in heaven for about two weeks when Betty called me into her room. "Sit down, I have a message for you. I just got in meditation that you are supposed to go to that Flower of Life Workshop. Bruce and I will watch the boys so you can go."

I thanked her for the message – she was doing what I had done for her in the past. I said, "I thank you for the message but I don't choose to spend $444.00 to sit for seven days and watch videos about sacred geometry and learn a left brained meditation. I want to see more of the island."

Betty was insistent, "Just go to see the free introduction. Meet Rebecca, meditate on it, and then decide." I did want to meet Rebecca and it couldn't hurt to spend one evening at a free talk. So I went.

When I got back that evening I told Betty, "You were right. As I watched the film it became clear that this workshop is not what we thought it was. I have decided to go."

Then Betty, who had gotten more guidance while I was gone, said, "I received guidance that I should go with you. Even though it's not my preference either, I have decided to go if the funds are made available, and Bruce is delighted at the prospect of having the boys all to himself. They are already planning what they want to do without us." The funds were made available for both of us to attend. Betty arranged an exchange for her admission and I was allowed credit and could pay monthly whatever was possible. The next week I found myself sitting next to Betty at the workshop and Bruce was watching the boys and having fun. I was there, but I still didn't know why.

The workshop was incredible, not at all what I had originally thought. We were told that in our sleep, Drunvalo would visit us in the astral. If we would ask, he would teach us even more. The entire first day was spent on the true history of the planet and how it came to be created. That night when I went to bed, I asked the teacher to come and tell me more. Above my bed a huge Orca whale appeared. Being very much awake, my first thought was, "I'm glad this is in the astral. He is huge." Then I heard over and over the words, "I am Orkeon and *you are Orkeon. You are Orkeon.*" It didn't stop until I had written the name down. I guess I wasn't supposed to forget who I was. Then I went out of my body. I was hanging on to this whale, as we went through the portals, belly to belly, swimming through the dimensions. Rings of color and bright light surrounded us. Waves of energy would come and go as everything around seemed to push us effortlessly forward.

All night long I was schooled in the true history of the world. At one point I complained, "I've heard enough. I sat all day listening to this stuff."

The whale replied, *"Then why did you ask to hear more?"*

In class the next day I mentioned to Rebecca what had happened. She laughed and said, "That was no ordinary whale that was Drunvalo. He often appears as a whale in the astral."

Wednesday was our day off from the workshop. Bruce planned to take us to a Ha-i-ou – sacred site of the islanders. Even though the workshop was rewarding, I was glad not to be watching any more videos, and looked forward to exploring a part of the island that we hadn't yet experienced.

To get to the Ha-i-ou we had to go through a cave. There were authentic cave paintings inside. The large opening at each end of the cave made it possible to easily see them. We walked through to the other side and entered a lush rain forest.

This was the side of the island that got the most rain. It had been sunny in Princeville when we left the condo, but it was raining here. This seemed strange since one could drive from one end of the island to the other in just thirty minutes. But this weather was typical for Kauai. It rained most of the time on one end of the island and on the other the sun usually shined. We saw rainbows and waterfalls everywhere which added to mystery and beauty everywhere one looked.

The enclosure we entered was like a tiny island in itself –

completely surrounded by mountains and only accessible through the cave we had just come through. If you walked in what seemed like a straight line, you would eventually end up where you started; at the entrance to the cave you came in from. At the opposite end of the circle, there was a huge cave that was pitch dark inside. In front of the cave there was an enormous tree which had been blown down in a devastating hurricane which hit the island two years before. The roots from the tree were used like an altar. Rocks wrapped in tea leaves were left as offerings, as was the spiritual custom. Flowers and various objects adorned the tree. It had become a focal point marking the entrance to the cave. The amazing thing was that the tree was still alive even though its roots were out of the ground and high above our heads.

Bruce and I decided to go into the cave. Betty and the boys refused to go in because it was so dark. That wasn't going to stop us. So we just walked in until we couldn't see our hands in front of our faces. It wasn't until the sound of water could be heard, and we got the strange feeling that there was no earth in front of us, that we both stopped simultaneously.

"Bruce wouldn't it be great if we had a flashlight or even a match so we could feel safe about exploring further?" He agreed. Then in a joking way, I put my hand up to the ceiling and proclaimed, "I am light. I am light. I am light." I used my breath to emphasize each statement. Immediately the cave lit up. Bruce and I – who could now see one another – looked at each other in amazement.

Then from behind us we heard, "Hey Jon, let's go in. Mom

lit up the cave." The boys ran in to play in front of us. The cave now seemed as bright as a day in the sun.

As we looked down, just inches from our feet, we saw a two foot drop with a small stream that trickled through the cave. I breathed a sigh of relief that we hadn't stumbled and fallen.

In complete denial that it had been I who lit the cave up, we talked about the logical possibilities which were few. I reasoned that the sun must have come out. There must be a hidden hole in the top of the cave that allowed the light to come in.

After about thirty minutes I was getting bored. There wasn't much to see after all. So I turned to leave the cave which had remained bright as day all that time. As I walked out the light seemed to follow and when I looked back, the cave was pitch-black. The boys didn't have to be told to come. As it got dark they ran out.

Outside, Betty was patiently waiting and a little damp from the rain. "Did the sun come out while we were in there?" I asked.

"No. It rained the whole time. What took you so long?"

The next day we returned to the workshop. It was time to have some fun. The information was not as heavy or left brained. The right brain would be exercised now and I was more comfortable in that territory. There were stories and adventures to hear about. Drunvalo told of a trip he had taken to the Great Pyramid in Egypt. In his adventure he had been given guidance to do specific things in preparation for something but he wasn't told what.

He had been taught by Thoth, an immortal being, who had appeared to him, and given the instructions. He was told by Thoth where to go, and what to do and say, while in a tunnel that was deep in the heart of the Great Pyramid. So Drunvalo traveled all the way to Egypt, got special permission to go into this off-limits tunnel, crawled on his hands and knees, and said the special words Thoth had given him. He blew out the candle and lay in the darkness with a few other people, waiting for something to happen. At first he had his eyes closed as he might in meditation. When he opened them the tunnel was lit up. He waited and waited for something big to happen. Then he asked Thoth if anything was going to happen? Thoth's reply was, *"Isn't it enough that you lit up the tunnel?"*

Immediately I thought of what had happened in the cave the day before. My response had been just like Drunvalo's – so what? If I had any doubt before about whether or not to be in this workshop, it had disappeared. This couldn't just be a coincidence.

Three years later I found myself as a Flower of Life Facilitator, giving a workshop at the place where our journey had begun; Swannanoa. I showed the tape of Drunvalo telling his story of lighting up the tunnel. Then I got guidance to stop the tape and tell the group about the cave in Hawaii. I hesitated, not wanting to seem boastful, but the guidance was strong. So I started to tell the story. First I had to tell a little about Bruce and Betty. There was a large picture window in the room where we were. As I said their names, I saw them walking across the lawn. I thought they were still in Hawaii. I said to the group, "You can meet them in person. I'll let them tell you what happened. Here they come now." Introductions were made and Bruce was happy to verify my story of lighting up the cave. What timing by the Universe! We were all amazed.

Back in Hawaii on the last day of the workshop, Bruce and I

were standing on the cliff behind the condo where we were staying. As we looked out over the ocean we saw a rainbow. This wasn't unusual as rainbows were abundant on the island. This one was different from any we had ever seen. It came from a single, round, puffy cloud which was all alone in a clear sky. Extending from the bottom of this cloud was a beam of rainbow light that shined its light deep into the waters below where dolphins swam. It was as if the cloud held a flashlight and was shining it into the ocean. The light in this rainbow was very vibrant and strong. One could see its color extend down to the floor of the sea. It reminded me of the rainbow which a small child and her teddy bear had ridden on in the past. It also reminded me of the recent out of body experience with Drunvalo – Orkeon.

In the workshop the day before we had been discussing the dolphins and their origins. Theories about dolphins actually coming from other worlds were discussed. One theory claimed that dolphins had the ability to come and go on rainbow beams of light. Could this be one of those portals to the other worlds? I don't know for sure about that, but I do know what I saw.

The month was gone and our visit to paradise was almost over. Just three days before we were to leave, on the last day of the workshop, Jon had a terrible accident. Betty was friends with Jeanie who had a son Jon's age. The boys wanted to play together that day and Jeannie offered to watch them. I thought it would be all right to let him play with this new friend. Jon was experimenting with model rocket fuel and sulfur from a chemistry set that was in their garage. He lit the fuel and the sulfur blew up in his face. Over half of his face was burned, with some first degree burns. They rinsed his face immediately in the shower and put aloe vera on the wounds.

When I arrived late that night not knowing anything had happened, I was greeted by my son whose face looked like raw ground beef. I was angry that they hadn't done anything to help Jon. I called the emergency poison control number; maybe they would know what we should do. They were very helpful. Since it had been several hours already, it would be all right to wait till morning to take him to a doctor. He was in a lot of pain and they recommended an over-the-counter pain medication. There was a problem; Jon had always refused to swallow pills but pills were all that were available. Even though the pain was severe, he was still unable to get the pills down. That night I reminded him of the regressions that we had done together when he had been much younger. He was able to relax a bit and I guided him into a deep state of meditation. Jon was in pain but his greatest concern was his appearance. He was a good-looking young man before the accident and was afraid of what he would look like now. I was aware of this and as part of the meditation; I took him to a healing place. There were healing angels who would take away his pain. I said, "If you believe it, in one week your scabs will come off and your face will be completely healed with no scarring." His breathing was easy now and he drifted off to sleep – the pain must have subsided.

In the morning we went to a local doctor who also practiced alternative medicine. The pain was gone and Jon was now complaining of intense itching. The doctor looked at Jon's face and said, "These wounds are already healing. What did you do to speed up the healing process?"

I said, "Guided Imagery and Reiki." He was familiar with both so a lot of explanation was not needed. It was wonderful to have a doctor who understood our efforts and didn't judge them.

He said, "Normally I would prescribe an antibiotic and special ointment, however I don't think that is necessary now. He must keep the wounds clean and uncovered. Use this soap. I'll write a prescription for the antibiotics but you needn't fill it unless you see signs of infection."

Jon's face did look a lot better than the day before but he still looked scary. His eyebrows and eyelashes had been burned off as well as some of the hair on his forehead. There were large craters; some as big as a half inch across that went deep into his face like huge pockmarks. The bits of sulfur had burned through all the layers of skin. When Jon left the room, the doctor told me that his face would probably be scarred permanently. I was glad that Jon didn't hear that. He felt bad enough as it was.

It was time to go back to the mainland. We said goodbye to Bruce and Betty and boarded the plane. Jon kept a baseball cap which Bruce had given him well down over his face and put up the collar of his jacket that was too warm to be wearing. He sank down in the seat and tried to be invisible. All that remained now were our vivid memories of this mystical island and the uncertainty of what we would find in the underground garage and the Los Angeles Airport.

It had been comforting having my good friends help with the trip from the east coast to the west coast – less intimidating. Now it was time to be by myself with the boys. We weren't sure what to expect in California because of the severe earthquake which had been centered near the area we were returning to. When we got off the plane in Los Angeles, we didn't know if we still had a car, and if we did, if the roads were open to drive on. We checked at an information desk and found out that only the roads north of the airport were closed. All the roads to the south were undamaged, and since that was the way we must travel, this was great news. We called the motel and were told that there had been no damage there either. We had been spared any inconvenience. Our guardian angels must have been on overtime. I was glad I hadn't worried unnecessarily.

We went back to the desert and even though we were all alone we spent most of our time camping at the dry lake that we loved so much and where the music of the spheres was still playing a nightly concert. The only difference was that now I got to sleep in the queen-size bed which was much more comfortable but lonely. The boys and I continued to play canasta by candlelight and build campfires. They now preferred to stay in the wilderness without electricity and had looked forward to the freedom they found there. We picked up Star and Lady who acted like they wanted to stay longer at the pet resort with their new friends. They were happy to see us but I could tell they had a good time too. Star started up her nightly conversations with the coyotes once more and we settled in to our little island in the desert.

One morning as I was waking, Jon called out, "Mom, come quick!" I was a little alarmed not knowing why he would be so excited. He was still in bed and there on his pillow was a huge scab. It had been exactly one week since his face was severely burned. The scab had come off in one big chunk and it lay there on his pillow. He ran to the mirror to look at his face. It was a miracle – a burst of faith! There were no scars, no craters – just pink and tender soft flesh. His eyebrows were filling in and the eyelashes were growing back. He looked as if he had a slight sunburn. To this day, one would never know anything had happen to his face. It looks perfectly normal.

A few years later during his first year in college; my handsome son, Jon, was in an almost fatal car accident. I received a call from the trauma unit at the Providence, Rhode Island hospital. The doctor was talking but I heard my angels telling me everything would be all right. I was allowed to talk to him on the phone as they were transporting him to the trauma unit. The doctor allowed me to talk him through a guided visualization in which I reminded him of the miracle of his face, assuring him once more that if he believed it, we would walk out of that hospital together in one week – and that is just what we did.

I flew to Providence that day. When I arrived I was told by the doctors, "He is in serious condition. He may have to have his spleen removed. It has been torn in three pieces. We are trying to reduce the bleeding and if it doesn't stop soon, he will need surgery to save his life. Your son is very fortunate to be with us. He also has a severe concussion and is now in a coma. There are three broken vertebrae in his back. We are doing all we can to stabilize him." As the doctor spoke, the angels were also giving me instructions.

As I prayed, my mind flashed to when Jonathan was born. He was two months early and only four pounds. He was immediately taken from me. A helicopter flew him to Baltimore and a special care unit. Before my husband and I left the hospital to drive to Baltimore, just hours after I gave birth, we had to name him for his birth certificate. My husband decided that his name should be Jonathan. I didn't care much for the name, but after looking up the meaning of it in my names book, I changed my mind. The definition was *a gift from God.* I prayed to God and the Angels, "Please don't take this wonderful gift back so soon."

I was allowed to see Jonathan. He was hooked up to monitors, tubes and wires. I prayed and called on the angels. Immediately, the room filled with golden light. I was guided to put my hands over his body and send the Reiki energy to him. His body seemed to become liquid. I was told not to put my hand into his body to try to fix anything myself. The numbers on the monitors were changing and his vitals were becoming more stable. I was left alone for one hour, a long time in this situation.

Then I called on the help of my spiritual family. Geoffrey and Diana Bullington were, at that moment, also saying prays with the group I was a part of. As it happened, their monthly group session was meeting on that day. I have learned never to underestimate the power of group prayer.

The nurse came in to take a sample of Jon's blood. She checked the monitors and said, "He is much more stable. When we get this blood work back we will let you know if he has to have his spleen removed." At the same time the angels were saying, "He will be fine." I continued to send him light and love and a few minutes later she came back and said, "I am really amazed. We rarely see such high blood counts in this unit. Looks like he will keep his spleen." I was relieved but not surprised.

The police took me to see the car. They said, "It's a miracle he survived. He had his seat belt on and it apparently failed. If it hadn't he would have been crushed. Fortunately he was somehow found in the passenger seat." When I saw the car I could hardly believe my eyes. There was only crushed and twisted metal on the driver's side where the van had broadsided his car.

One week later, Jonathan, my gift from God, was released from the hospital and I took him home. Today Jon has just one small scar on his face from this accident. I have even more faith in Spirit.

Back in California, our family had grown closer and we now decided what to do and where to stay based on everyone's guidance and desires. We stayed in the Borrego Desert by ourselves for about a month. I asked Jon and Mike what we should do next. "Do you want to make our new home here in California or did you see another place that you liked better on our trip?"

They surprised me with their reply. "Let's go back to Virginia and build our home on that land we bought before we left."

Since the first offer to buy the land just the day after the closing papers were signed, two more offers had come in the mail from people who were interested in buying the 18 ½ acres that I had bought in the Blue Ridge Mountains of Virginia. These offers had come to our general delivery post office box in the Borrego Desert. I had been tempted to sell to get the extra funds, and now I was happy that I had chosen not to.

We were all homesick for those beautiful mountains and the Shenandoah Valley. Nothing we had seen could compare. Not even Hawaii or Disneyland appealed to the boys. And of course, there were the friends and family we had left on the east coast that made the idea even more appealing. We had seen a lot, and Virginia still looked like our best choice in every way. We had discovered that it wasn't the place that mattered; it was the people who made it home. Our hearts were in Virginia. That would be our new home.

We journeyed back across the country arriving on Easter Sunday. An architect was found and we built an eight sided house on those beautiful wooded acres on the side of Afton Mountain.

Jon chose to go back to public school, and for the next two years I continued to home-school Mike, who had absolutely no desire to return to conventional life. These boys have in the past, and probably will in the future, be total opposites.

We had gained new insights in our travels and adventures. We faced our new lives with a richer consciousness, living in the moment, and creating the last chapters of this book.

Chapter 16

Jon, Mike, Star, Lady, and I have settled in comfortably to this more ordinary way of living. The miracles and inner dimensional journeys have never stopped. The words flow with less interference and it is easier to integrate the lessons I am writing about into my everyday life thus walking my talk.

Challenges continue to arise but our way of responding to them has changed. There is more focus on finding what we may learn from each experience, rather than dwelling on the pain that may accompany it, playing the role of the victim. In this chapter it is my desire, before going on to new stories, to share with you some of the insights that were given to assist me with those more challenging yet rewarding parts of the tapestry.

A message from Spirit – February 9, 1997

It is indeed a pleasure to once again have the opportunity to communicate through you. All is in readiness for the grand event of our reunion with the one true Source of All. We stand by patiently waiting, as only God, Creator, Source, which ever name you would choose, knows when this shall be. In a sense, in the all-time, it has already occurred, this merging. For if you are in the past, present, and future of the moment, all creation has already been welcomed home. This is the true destiny of all. It is like the miracle of birth to death. The blossoming of a tiny seed or the rain that falls back to the oceans. There is a process, a cycle, or as you may say, a continuing. Nothing ever dies, and nothing ever remains exactly the same. All is continually being recreated, out of itself, to new levels of awareness. This path, from the beginning, has always led back to just one place. Some may call this place the golden city of light, or heaven, the redemption, the rapture. Many explanations or descriptions have been offered in many sacred books. They are there simply to prepare you for what is to come.

This is a time for great rejoicing and celebration, not a time of loss, or separation. All shall be united again and in a much happier creation. Mankind has created from the wave of the original fall from grace, a world foreign from its origin. As all things must return to their origins, so too will your planet return home.

This is also a time to cultivate faith, to pray and commune, in whatever way you choose, with the Creator. It is a time to remember who you are, why you came, and take action. Fulfill the prophecies you were destined to create. All is in your hands, and your hands are held by God. Fear not, for it is a simple task. When each of you join hands together, pray, and love all things unconditionally, your prayers shall be answered. They shall not be answered by a wrathful, judgmental God, but rather a loving, compassionate truth that has always been there, patiently waiting for you to remember who you are, why you came, allowing you to get on with the coming back together again.

Within each of you is the power of Source. In the past, you have been in fear of your own power and have hidden it. You deny your origin, yet in your Bible you are taught that you are created in God's image. Would God's image be powerless? Maybe God has amnesia. Now this is a silly notion, is it not? Maybe not so silly though. Are you not a part of God and do you not feel powerless to do something to save the environment you have created? So we say to you, remember who you are. Trust your power to heal and return the consciousness of the planet back to its original pristine perfect state. Just start with your own being. Take responsibility for yourself, love yourself, do not judge where you are. In the moment, commune with your God-self. Reclaim your birthright to be as God, united, within Source.

You my be saying to yourself, "But I am not God." If you believe that God is a separate being outside of yourself and you are not worthy to be in God's presence, then of course the thought of even comparing one's self to God would be an outrageous, egotistical thought. Is it not just as egotistical to tell God that you are not who God says you are? It is appropriate that the one who writes this has been, through marriage, given the name Gedeon. Look to the story of how Gideon doubted God. He demanded of God that he be given not one but three different miracles, to prove he was worthy to be who God said he was. Is this not the ultimate ego? He put himself above his own Creator. It is only natural to have disbelief in this illusionary world that you reside. Many of you have been taught from birth to believe in a world that says God is separate, or has favorites, or judgments. That is why in these times, it is so important to have faith in what the God – that is within each

*of you – is saying. Follow that guidance. Do not doubt that God
exists within you. Everything exists within God. Claim your divine
right to be powerful and reunite all of God's consciousness together
once again. Be co-creators, surrender all ego or fear, and embrace
only love. Live the truth, a truth that knows all that ever existed was
the Creator, God, or Source, the union of the oneness within and
without all. So be it!*

Union, Eternal Bliss

Union, eternal bliss,
The marriage of the mother's kiss,
To the father's embrace in the waiting place.

Union, eternal bliss,
Memories of arms outstretched,
Embraces and hugs of welcome and love.

Union, eternal bliss,
Reminding me of God's sweet breath,
Lingering in my lungs and chest.

Union, eternal bliss,
Coming again to this place in time,
Blending and merging all as one.

Union, eternal bliss,
Doubt and fear all erased,
Love and joy stand in their place.

Union, eternal bliss,
One within the one,
All time – all space.

Union, eternal bliss,
Touch God's eager fingertips,
And rest in the arms of Creation.

Message from Spirit, March, 1997

Greetings beloved. We are here with you once again. Our purpose for writing these words shall soon become apparent. There is some distraction in the process of communication. The energy of the computer interrupts the flow. If you wish to just use a pencil and paper, you may find it much easier to communicate with us. However, if it is your wish to continue in this manner, we shall accommodate you by speaking louder or more directly through your fingers. Allow the keyboard of the computer to become an extension of your senses. Let go of thinking and just allow what would flow into your consciousness to be translated through your fingers and onto the screen. Trust that this new method is just as effective as what you are accustomed to.

Question – Do you have any suggestions to assist me in becoming thin, healthy, and more youthful?

Your focus should be not so much on the physical but more on what lies at the center of your being. Caught in the illusion of the polarity, you have fixed your attention on the symptoms and not the causes of your problems. If you get a thorn in your foot, do you treat the infection that may be caused by the thorn without removing it? You would not leave that thorn sticking out of your skin without removing it first before treating the wound.

The thorn is a bit more obvious but no less effective in treating the cause of your problems. So we say to you, whenever approaching a problem, first find the thorn and remove it. Then the body can get on with healing itself as it was naturally designed to do. We know that you do not have visible thorns sticking out of your flesh. If they were obvious, no doubt you would remove them immediately. We speak of the hidden arrows that have penetrated your being at its very core of existence.

In truth, there is no disease. It simply does not exist. When you think of God do you see a being with a cold? The illusion you have created pulls you into the belief that because you are human, you must suffer physical illness. Of course, what you believe, you create. The thorn that you must remove is the one that festers – the belief that you are separate from God. Once that thorn is taken away you may exist in a state of grace.

If you should be successful in removing the thorn or separation, do not be quick to judge others who may not be successful in obtaining perfect health. Remember there is purpose in all. Their purpose for being in the flesh may well be to suffer the illusion of the illness. If you did not feel the thorn, would you even try to remove it?

Judgment itself is a thorn that pierces the very heart of God. God who does not judge, but patiently waits and empowers you to find the thorn yourself. The gift God gives is the acceptance of whatever your choice may be.

So the choice is yours to make. Find the source of separation and acknowledge that it does not exist, or continue to exist in the illusion that the pain is necessary because you are separate from God and do not deserve to live in a state of grace.

We know this is not what you wanted to hear. It is much easier to go to the doctor and have him prescribe some drug to cure the problem. This is successful in that moment in removing the pain on the surface. If you do not address the reason for the problem, it will just manifest again and again until you realize that it is trying to speak to you. The illness is telling you that it is there and it does not belong in God's body. If you ignore it, it will just scream louder and louder, creating even more evidence of its presence until you can deny it no longer. We say to you, do not wait until the thorn has become a threat to your physical existence. Remove it now and become whole once more!

Thorn

Locked deep within the heart of humankind,
A tiny thorn did God first find.
Seek out its source and pluck it out.
Heal the wound that it has made,
Remembering the state of God's grace.

For a while, this advice from Spirit fell on deaf ears. I realized that the thorn had festered and the judgment of myself and the medical profession had stopped me from having that thorn removed. I decided to undergo a long overdue operation to remove my uterus.

It took a while, six months, to get up the courage to do something about having this thorn taken out. Of course, as always, there was a great deal of help along the way –God's weavers. My friends and teachers, Geoffrey and Diana, as well as all the members of our monthly group, would become my extended family and help to weave this important part of the tapestry. And then, there was my physical vehicle that *demanded* attention.

Just after my husband departed and when my son Michael was about one year old, I was diagnosed with uterine fibroids. My doctor said this was a common condition in women and as long as my health wasn't at issue, there was no need to have surgery. For years this thorn was ignored because the physical complaints were minor.

The symptoms grew so slowly that I got accustomed to the minor problems associated with the fibroids. Over the next ten years, there was a slow and steady decline of my physical body; more and more excess weight, more and more heavy bleeding, less and less energy, and a larger and larger stomach. I assumed some of the symptoms were caused by menopause. As the physical condition worsened there was further denial necessary. I can remember thinking, "I look and feel just like I did before the delivery of my children."

I was supposed to be a spiritual healer and a teacher. Why was I not able to help myself? How could this be? Blaming myself, feelings of doubt and low self-esteem pulled me down to a very dark corner of the tapestry. This separated me from that very thread that would have helped me; seeing and listening through the soul. Opportunities for clients dropped off; there were no workshops or private healing sessions. (One may only give what one has to give.) All focus and attention must go to healing myself. The more I fought the obvious solution to the problem, the more energy it took to keep up the fight. Because of this immersion in the pattern of illusion I had forgotten how to listen to God and was just surviving. I had forgotten how to create that happy, flowing, loving, energetic, and healthy tapestry.

I was tough, and sure that *God* was going to heal me – not some *surgeon*. But I was also blind and deaf to the help that was available to me from Spirit, including the message about the thorn. Learning to receive was one of the lessons. (*All is in divine order. No part of the tapestry is a mistake. What has been called a mistake is a tool used to create the next part of the tapestry.*)

It was the physical body that finally put me on my knees, and in great pain compelled me to take action. Now there was no way to ignore the thorn; my body was talking to me. I could ignore Spirit – turn off the messages, but not the physical body. There was no choice but to listen to that. After a visit to the doctor I was immediately sent to the hospital for tests. My white blood cell count was high and there was fever, nausea, and extreme pain – all the symptoms of an acute appendix. The cysts in my uterus had gotten so large they were bursting and flooding the body with toxins. Every inch of my being ached with pain. For six weeks diarrhoea and heavy bleeding drained what little energy remained, leaving me depressed and feeling *separate* from everything.

The great detail of this ordeal was not written for sympathy, but to paint a vivid picture of what one may create when separating one's self from the tapestry. One is then free to find one's soul.

You've heard that old expression, "The bigger they are, the

harder they fall." Here one may also say, "The more wilful they are, the more willing they become." There was no choice but to become a willing partner with a surgeon.

When the doctor told me it wasn't my appendix, I was actually upset. It would have been all right to have emergency surgery for a life threatening condition. I was surprised at my reaction and realized it was time to stop the judgment. Before that realization, I was in total denial of this judgment. For five years, every possible treatment, herb, faith healer, and alternative method was tried. None of them took away the cysts. After leaving the hospital that day, I made the decision to see a surgeon and get this over with so I could live again as a co-creator and not just a survivor.

The word "failure" wasn't in my vocabulary. I was determined to discover *why* it was in divine order to have surgery. The focus was on creation again. What a great opportunity the universe – God – had given me! The gift had been there all along but I wasn't ready to receive it.

It was during this time that Geoffrey and Diana Bullington came into the pattern of this creation in a profound way. They had started a class which met once a month on a Saturday. I worked every Saturday and hadn't been able to join them. A new Sunday class was beginning. Now I could attend. Having first been introduced to this dynamic couple through my friend Betty, I had grown to trust their guidance. For four years I worked privately on the phone with Geoffrey, who lived in Kentucky. We also meet on a yearly basis at the University of Science and Philosophy's homecoming event at Swannanoa. Whenever major decisions or a crisis arose Geoffrey and Diana were always there to listen and lend moral support. Their guidance was always helpful and empowering. This was important since on many occasions there were no other adults who understood or could offer their level of advice.

Their class became a lifeline to my soul. There is a saying that the master comes when the student is ready. At each level of my soul's training this has proven to be the case. It was time to listen again and I am glad that I listened and chose the teachers that I did. My teachers proved to be not just Geoffrey and Diana but each person in the group, and extended soul family.

Once the decision was made to have the surgery, I had about three months to prepare myself for the event. If it had to be done, I wanted to be sure to make the most of it – to benefit and learn from it as much as possible. I was listening to God again and focusing on creating a positive experience, not just for me, but for everyone involved. This was my prayer and it was answered.

Geoffrey gave me a forty minute visualization on tape, a form of mediation that I would listen to every day for six weeks. It was designed for me to create the least resistance in my body and assisting in letting go of any fears or doubts that may surface. Parts of it included envisioning the operation, seeing everything going perfectly, the surgeon's hands full of light, and guided by God. All of the staff involved in the procedure are seen as happy and working as an efficient, loving, nurturing unit.

The tape was created in the All Time where the surgery was already taking place, even though I was listening before the actual event. We travelled within the cellular level of my being and talked to the tissue that would be cut, preparing the skin for the surgeon's scalpel, allowing the body to open with less trauma and pain. My blood vessels were told to close and seal off as they were severed so there would be no excess bleeding. Each nerve that was cut was insulated from pain. My brain was programmed that there would be no excess bleeding or pain and my recovery would be swift and easy.

During the meditation, I envisioned the surgeon removing only that which was necessary and taking every part of the thorn that had threatened to rip the fabric of the tapestry. As she cut through each cord to the womb that no longer served me, I felt lighter and lighter, and free of the programming I had received in my mother's womb over fifty years ago when she was giving birth to me.

It was so clear. I had taken on my mother's thorns that she had gotten from her mother in her womb. It was now easy to see how each generation passed down through the womb the illusion as well as the positive. In unconditionally loving my mother while she was carrying me, I had taken on her pain, her fears, and her emotions so that she would not have to experience them. It was now time to give birth to a new me and stop enabling my mother. As I reconstructed the circumstances of my birth and what my mother must have been going through emotionally, it became easier for me to understand why I had struggled with certain issues in this lifetime. By cutting the cords in the meditation, I was letting go of my mother's pain. It was no longer mine.

Viewing the operation now as an opportunity to heal more than just a physical ailment, the meditation expanded to include altering old belief systems and patterns in the tapestry that had been interfering with the flow of the weave. The old programming I had received in my mother's womb about my weight, relationships, poverty issues, and much more were addressed with the flip of a switch in my brain.

During the meditation we went into the cellular level of my brain. While under anaesthesia, I envisioned myself flipping off all the switches in my brain in the dendrite field. Then all the switches were turned on again with new circuitry creating new neuropath ways to my brain. This was an opportunity to recreate belief systems, old programming, and much more that I hadn't yet discovered.

A female doctor was recommended as an excellent surgeon who had a lot of experience with this specific procedure. We met and had a good rapport. It was important that I feel comfortable sharing what I was doing to prepare for the surgery. She was quite open-minded and interested in the meditation. I chose her to be my partner in this project and was now looking forward to the event.

My faith had been restored and the memory of something Spirit said years ago in *Kingdoms of Light* came to comfort me – a Universal Truth – *Everything is in divine order.* All that I had learned and taught was flooding back to assist me in weaving the threads of this operation into my tapestry.

The soul of the earth and the animal kingdoms were sending me encouraging messages too. The day before the operation, as I stood on the front porch of my home, a blur of wings hovered inches from my face. It hovered there for a few minutes. The object was so close I couldn't focus on it. It was only as the object flew off that I discovered it was a hummingbird. This was a message. The hummingbird is delicate yet it has great strength and endurance. Its wings move in a figure eight which signifies power and strength. Joy is the hummingbird's message and I saw this as a positive sign and great blessing. The timing was perfect – the day before the surgery. Minutes later upon entering the kitchen, on the other side of the window just a foot away, there was another hummingbird. It hovered there for a few minutes looking at me through the glass. That evening I drove to the top of Afton Mountain to pick Jon up from his job. Another hummingbird flew over to me and again hovered in front of me. Three hummingbirds in one day. I hadn't seen that many all year. Each time they came, I felt great joy and an inner knowing that all would be fine the next day.

I honoured my womb which was to be removed by thanking it for all the years it had been of service. It had housed and nourished both my children. I told my uterus that it had served me well but it was time for it to leave. This was a way of totally letting go of all self-judgment by not judging that part of me that was diseased. Instead, my uterus was being honoured for its service and acknowledged for the role that it was playing in the pattern of the Creator. Without it, I would not have discovered the thorn or had this opportunity to grow.

The anaesthesiologist allowed me to wear my head phones so I could play my meditation tape during the operation. I had no fear at all, placing myself in the hands of the Creator and all the co-creators in the operating room – seeing God in everyone. I completely let go with the knowledge that whatever the outcome of the surgery, *all was in divine order.*

The surgery was a success and without exception, every part of my visualization was created and placed firmly and lovingly in the pattern of the weave. I was given a private room (which I hadn't asked for) with a beautiful view of the mountains I loved so much. The surgery had taken considerably longer than expected – over four hours. When the doctor came to see me she said, "You really got you money's worth." – An affirmation of abundance. She explained, "You had acute endometriosis and I had to carve your uterus out because it was glued to everything around it. I left one ovary but the other had to be removed. I really don't know how you could have lived with this for so long." Despite all the manipulation of my internal anatomy, there was little pain and little bleeding. The next day I got up and walked to the opposite end of the 3rd floor to see the babies in the maternity ward – how appropriate having just given birth to a new self.

Three days after the surgery, I was released from the hospital. That morning a beautiful rainbow appeared outside my hospital window. It seemed as if this rainbow was an acknowledgment of the birth of a new me and a new beginning. I was reminded of the double rainbow Betty and I had seen years ago when we started off in our new friendship, and of the journey we made together listening only to God and having faith in our guidance.

The only time I felt any physical pain was when I tried to do too much. This was also put into the meditation so that I wouldn't overdo – which in the past had been a pattern. As soon as I got home I had to stop the pain medication, as was having a reaction to it. Even without the medication I discovered that there was no pain.

Violet, a class member and good friend, insisted on taking me to the hospital, picking me up at five in the morning. She then joined other members of the class at my home. They worked together, cleaning the house from top to bottom while I was in surgery. Others brought food so I didn't have to cook when I returned home. I felt their love and support and was able to receive it. My youngest son, Mike, took care of me the first few days I was home, answering yet another prayer. We were able to strengthen our relationship and it gave him pride in himself because he was now valued as *my* caretaker.

This was a time to receive. There was no choice. In the future I would see illness as a messenger – a signal – the body saying, "Receive." This also had been about balance and the scales were tipped too far in one direction. Why deny someone else the joy of giving to me? How selfish. My physical body was out of alignment because I did more giving than receiving, and balance creates a healthier body, mind and soul.

In *no time* I was back to normal and actually feeling better than I had for a long time. I was even able to attend Geoffrey's and Diana's class that same month, and never had to miss a meeting.

During the six week check-up the doctor said she was impressed with my rapid recovery, and the positive effect my preparation and state of mind had made. She said, "We made a good team." This planted a new seed in my mind. Could I possibly be working in the future with surgeons, helping others prepare for

surgery? Was this another thread that lead to a whole new tapestry?
The decision hasn't been made yet about this. One thing is for sure
– if I hadn't had the experience there wouldn't be a possibility to do
that type of work.

The following message has been included at this point in the
text. It was written during the time period of the previous
experience of surgery.

October 28, 1997

It is six in the morning and my body doesn't know it – being programmed to awaken at seven. We just set the clocks back an hour for daylight savings time. My internal alarm clock went off on schedule. The dogs are also a bit confused but the sun must know for it has yet to rise.

Eternal Autumn

Fall
 Is
  Here. *The leaves turn*
     Rust orange
         Golden
       Red.
   Falling and
     Separating. *Drifting*
       Windblown
         Through the air.
The leap

   Of faith awaits their fate.

Then gently
    Drifting
     Downward
      Spiral.
       Ever
        closer
        earth
   In   *grows*
    Mother's   *near.*
     arms
     now cradled softly as we go
      crunching – our foot steps hear.

A blanket of color now surrounds us,

Knee-deep in beauty of fallen souls.
Remember their love's leap into the darkness.
The faith of a billion stars is ours to hold.

In just one eternal moment of a creator's clock,
Time shall stand still forever more,
Forgetting heartbreak, disease, and aging,
Embracing youth, and love, and joy.

Here we stand knee deep in fall's hues,
Embracing one's eternal joy,
To find the alarm set within our souls.
Its ring shall be heard in the spring of the morn.

Our gaze goes up now to the bare limbs waving,
As they embrace and greet the air.
Under the surface, the buds they form,
With no remembrance of the cold, crisp, and bare.

How may we choose to be yet as the leaves of old; their
purpose not gone but transformed to become the star?
In this great cycle of love all of the focus seems on the new
beginning – though fall is never gone; just a remembrance of the All
– The season of the mind.

May each season be embraced and released to once more find the
beginning that never ends, and claim eternal faith and grace.

All has PURPOSE,
All is PRECIOUS,
All is ONE.

Chapter 17

One day while in the store, I bought an outdoor thermometer but had no idea just how hot it was going to get inside my home. I thought I was buying it for the outside porch to keep an eye on the cold temperatures that we had been having. That evening I stoked the fire just before I intended to go to bed. The previous night I had difficulty getting the wood to burn and not go out in the middle of the night. Not wanting to awaken to a cold house again, I put a bit too much of the very dry, seasoned oak in the stove, and the fire almost got out of control.

My fears rose and so did the anger at myself. How could I have been so dumb? The floor in front of the hearth was almost too hot to walk on and the cast-iron wood stove was orange red. As I watched the awesome power of the raging contained fire intense fear and emotion filled me. Because I had panicked, it never occurred to me to throw water on it. There was always the possibility of a call to the fire department. I went within and asked what must be done. A voice from within said, "Since you can't sleep, watch the fire and write." The following words came to me and as I wrote I noticed that the fire within as well as without calmed.

The fire rages within you. Are you not aware of why the flames burn so high? Is it not clear how much anger is bottled up within your being? Release that anger; find a way to acknowledge and express it before it destroys you. Embrace your anger. Do not judge or justify it. Acknowledge and thank it for helping you to know when others have violated your sacred space in some way. It is not bad to be angry. There is purpose in all. Remove the blinders you wear that keeps your anger bottled up.

What is it you wish to destroy – yourself? Of course not, but what is it this bottled up anger is destroying? Your peace, your harmony, your health, your essence are being threatened and lost. Scream, release, act out, let go – let your rage go! It is all right to be angry at injustice and bondage, rape and starvation, disease and the ill health of the planet. It is not all right to torture yourself with guilt, fear, or judgment. God is not guilty. God does not fear, and God is not in judgment. So, inasmuch as you embody a part of God how can you stay in guilt, fear, or judgment?

We say to you, strive to be ever present in God consciousness. Stand in God's strength – that gentle strength that is one with all creation. Do not stand in angry, fearful shoes. These do not serve you. They do not belong to God. Do not judge yourself for having put them on. Thank them for serving you as you walked your path with them and lovingly let them go. Your feet have grown out of them and they no longer serve you, for they no longer serve God.

Fire Rages Within
Flames of anger, hatred, woe,
Lick the air, fuel distress.
All consumed in fire's glow.

Molten lava lies below.
'Neath her surface rosy glow.
Rivers molten ever flow.
Life's blood, rivers, current, force.
God's redemption – Eternal Source.

Channel the power of your anger to the power of love.
See the river of anger being flooded with the river of compassion.
Hence the fires of Hell are drowned in the river of Love – God's
redemption.

My children have proven to be the greatest gift. That doesn't in any way mean that there have never been challenges in our relationships. On many occasions they challenge me to walk my talk.

Those who have survived the process, or are still involved in rearing teens in today's world, probably understand just how stressful life can get. It is difficult enough when there are two parents going through this age with just one child. Just think how difficult it must be as one parent with two teen-aged boys teamed up against you. I've always believed in the saying, "God never gives you more than you can handle." Some days I think God must have made a big mistake. Of course, God doesn't make mistakes. Since it was called to my attention in this book on a previous page that a part of God is in me, how could I, as part of God, have made such a big mistake?

My two little angels were testing me to the limit and I lost my temper. I won't go into details about what was said or done. Because of the argument, I flew into a rage that might have been heard miles away. I was so angry that I went out of control. The boys were shocked. How could she scream at us and lose control? We do it all the time but she's not supposed to do that!

They decided they had better get out of my way. God has no greater fury than a angry mother pushed beyond her threshold of tolerance! I claimed my power in that moment and accused my children of abuse. I told my children I would not be abused by them anymore. Because of the state I was in, and the way I presented this to them, I have no doubt they believed I was serious. They didn't choose to argue with me. In their flight they left me alone in the house. This was not the first time I had claimed my power and swore never to let this happen again. So why did it keep happening? Why did I continue to create this anger?

To calm down, I decided to write. I was still writing in longhand and then typing what I had written into the computer. I got out the hand written manuscript of the previous pages in this book and guess what was next to be typed? The pages on anger. Had I already forgotten what I had just written the day before? Reading this passage again was like reading it with a new brain. Since I was still in anger and already dealing with my self-judgment for losing control, the words took on a new level of meaning. For the first time it was clearer to me why this pattern was repeating.

I had been taught that there was no justification for anger, so I stuffed it. The guilt fed me something that was familiar. Even though it wasn't a pleasant experience, a part of me was addicted to it – addicted to anger and self-abuse.

I had heard this theory before but somehow, being in the moment of the anger and reading this passage gifted me with the ability to see the full impact of how powerfully this had played out in my life. I must stop judging myself, step out of the illusion, and see through the eyes of my soul. I thanked God for my anger and for the opportunity my children had provided for me to release it. Now, it was time to embrace the opportunity and step out of the abusive world I had woven in the past. If the occasion arose again, I would be the best "angry" that I could be. I would release the anger and in the moment, create a new pattern that served me in a more loving way and hence would serve all those around me.

Chapter 18

It's five in the morning and I am battling a cold. Of course there are the normal flu like symptoms. I am just an ordinary person so I feel terrible. With that in mind, why would I be up at five a.m. and writing? Most normal people would stay in bed as long as they could when they felt so miserable. Last night I put on a dolphin meditation tape that has helped me heal in the past. I read the first thirty-six pages of the book *Emissary of Light* by James F. Twyman, and then listened to his CD, which I had just purchased. Mike was also not feeling well so from time to time I got up to attend to his needs, and didn't fall asleep until one or two in the morning. I should be a little blurry-eyed. Surprise! Suddenly I sat up in bed still feeling pretty awful but with that familiar knowing inside that it was time to write. I got up, made a cup of ginger tea, took some homeopathic cold and flu remedies and got to work.

The quiet is so wonderful when even the chickens are asleep. Slight correction, I just heard the rooster crow. Guess the chickens aren't asleep either. I am reminded of how several years ago, perhaps more than several, I would be awakened in the middle of the night to write, when we lived at the Crystal Rainbow Center. I was having a battle with asthma then which has since disappeared. I would be awakened in a similar fashion. The memory of how the asthma would disappear as I wrote stopped me from rolling over and going back to sleep to escape the aches and pains of the flu. Instead I would listen and write. I am already feeling much better as the focus is now on creating and connecting with Source in the moment. Writing has always been my best medicine. There is no logical way to explain this phenomenon, but then who ever said the power of the mind was logical. What an ironic concept. The mind not being logical. Yet, it is the most undiscovered part of the anatomy.

I have shared with you the stories of my life that have given me faith, and written of miracles – bursts of faith. How does one sustain a state of grace, where miracles are expected? Perhaps we can discover the answer to this question by examining what was in place on some of the occasions when I was successful – living in a state of grace.

I was strongly guided to go to a book signing at the Quest Bookshop in Charlottesville. Being in a reclusive mood and coming down with this cold I really didn't want to go. The urge and the message were so strong that I went anyway. My prayer all day was if I was supposed to go this cleansing that seemed inevitable, the cold would be held back. I didn't want to spread whatever I might be getting with the people who would be there. The prayers were answered and it wasn't until my friends and I were driving home that my throat started to close up and the other symptoms started to flow once more. It is as if when the energy is high, disease can't exist. Wouldn't it be wonderful to have the ability to maintain that high energy forever? No more disease. It seems like a pipe dream but part of me knows this is our destiny. Some may call it enlightenment – being in a constant state of grace or Christ-consciousness. How many of us when we think of God, or Christ, or Buddha, think of them with a cold?

It wasn't clear who was going to speak or why Spirit thought it was so important for me to go. The guidance had been when *Kingdoms of Light* was written, not to clutter my mind with what had already been written. The message was to focus on what was automatically flowing through the stream of consciousness. Instead of reading I would place books like A *Course in Miracles*, Walter Russell's *The Universal One, The Keys of Enoch,* or the *Bible* under my bed. From time to time, I found myself quoting these books that I had never physically read. Later, I got curious after *Kingdoms of Light* was completed, so I opened them and read. As I flipped through these books that may have seemed so different and separate in content, I discovered something. They were all saying basically the same things. They all contained universal truths and were all a part of the universal tapestry. Each was a bridge from God-consciousness to human consciousness.

This event was a book signing and I would leave with yet another book to put under my bed. The author, James Twyman, was a very modest yet incredible man. As he played his guitar and sang peace prayers, the energy in the room soared. In no time at all my cold had disappeared completely. Everyone in the room was totally entranced and at the end of the song there was complete silence. Applause would have been inappropriate and broken the peace which had been created.

As I listened to James, I was hearing myself being a channel for the universal truth to groups and workshops I had given in the past – the basic truths that were common in all those books I had slept with and had even written. He exemplified the simplicity of St. Francis, so his message was simple and yet universal and all encompassing; see the God in everyone – a simple yet very powerful bridge to God-consciousness. To do that one must see through the soul.

James said he was a troubadour for peace and had sung all over the world. His book *The Emissary of Light* had recently been published. I heard him say things that also had been channeled through me. It seemed as if he was speaking directly to me. He told of how he had written his book in just two weeks and within a month found a literary agent and a publisher. I had been questioning how my book would be published. The answer was have faith and just keep writing.

One thing that stood out as he spoke were these questions, "Who am I?" and "Why was I chosen? How can I possibly get this message out to the world?" He said he was picked because he was an ordinary person and if an ordinary person could be chosen, then any other person in the world could be an emissary too. Part of the message was that we are all equal. We are not separate but one.

After the talk as I handed James my copy of his book to sign he said, "When I give a talk, I pick one person in the room to speak directly to. You were that person tonight." He signed my book by drawing a big heart and writing, "To Joyce – You're Ready!!!!"

It wasn't just my imagination that he was speaking directly to me. Who am I? I am every person in that room. I am you. The message was clear. If I would write it, they would read it. The book would be published. I am an emissary of light.

Two thousand years ago, the man, Jesus, was also an emissary, a humble carpenter. His message is finally being understood. The Christ is within each of us. We are the Christ, the children of God. We are the Buddha, we are Mohammed, we are Mother Mary, and Mother Teresa. We are ordinary people. We are God's love.

It is now seven o'clock. I have finished writing and my cold of course, having served its purpose, has disappeared. It is time to resume my ordinary life in an extraordinary way; focusing on the love and oneness of every person and thing that I touch today.

The Tapestry has expanded. New threads go out to draw together the tapestries of all nations and all people, all religions and beliefs – all one enormous *Universal Tapestry of Love as seen Through the Eyes of the Soul.*

"Oh Lord, make me an instrument of your peace. Oh Lord, make me an instrument of your peace..." Over and over these words echoed in my head. As my eyes opened in the still darkness this song that I had listened to on Jimmy's CD repeated over and over again; this simple lyric so powerful and compelling.

Spirit would often serenade me in the stillness. I often awaken to songs being sung that give messages or just make me feel good all over. Sometimes it is just a single voice singing and sometimes an entire angelic choir. The effect is always uplifting and inspiring.

Two things come to mind as this song vibrates through my being. One a story – they seem to be never-ending, the other, a t-shirt that Mike likes to wear.

In the mall one day, he showed me this shirt. It had printed on it these words, "I do what the voices in my head tell me to do." Even though I recognized that this was a sarcastic attempt at negative humor, we bought the shirt. In our minds the shirt wasn't saying what the makers of it had intended. It was for us about following our inner voice; the voice that nourished, guided, and uplifted.

I'm sure the person who conceived the idea of this shirt didn't know how we would interpret it. It was perfect. Mike, who loved to shock adults by being outrageous, could secretly be a messenger of light, while still playing his rebellious role with his peers. Since it is not the "in thing" for a teen boy, Mike covers up that tender, caring soul of his with a sandpaper mask. He is often embarrassed and afraid to share that which he believes is vulnerability. How many of us do the same because we are also afraid that our true nature, which is pure love, will be discovered and rejected? Our vulnerability is the greatest gift we possess, but sometimes we cover it with a mask of fear.

This brings us to the second story which is an example of living in a state of grace. This event took place near the center in Shenandoah. While driving down the road one morning I had to suddenly slam on the brakes. There, in the center of the road, stood an elderly, scruffy-looking man waving a dirty rag. The roads in that area are not flat. They wind and dip frequently. This man was at the bottom of a high hill and I didn't see him until I was almost on top of him. As I caught my breath after the sudden stop, I realized that the cars behind me attempting to stop would have even more difficulty and less warning than I had. Everything seemed to happen in seconds, yet time appeared to be stretched out as I watched the car behind me safely stop without hitting my car. I breathed a short sigh of relief and then another car came. As the distance and the warning got shorter and shorter for the next vehicles, I sat quietly in prayer watching a string of near accidents taking place behind me.

Some cars actually had to go into ditches to avoid the cars in front of them. Luckily a church parking lot was on the right, and some of the cars actually pulled off into the side road of this parking lot to escape a collision. The chain reaction continued until the cars that were having to stop reached the top of the hill. Then the oncoming traffic could see what lay ahead. Until this happened things were exciting.

It seemed a miracle that not one car was damaged. As the dust settled, people got out of their vehicles to check on other people in the cars that were in ditches. No one was hurt; just shaken up a bit. A man walked up to my window to talk to me so I rolled it down and calmly said, "Don't you think they should have put signs up on top of the hill to avoid this happening?" Still being in a state of shock, it hadn't occurred to me to be angry at anyone but after my words were spoken, the man next to my car flew into a violent rage. He was angry and there was no mistaking that. Now my prayers were directed in front of my car.

This poor old man was being attacked by the men who were getting out of the cars that were piled up behind me. He was part of a crew of men who were working on paving a private driveway.

They must have worked for a small company and not the state highway crew. No road signs had been posted as to the impending stop or work in progress. Not even a slow down or a caution sign could be seen. The only warning was a dirty rag being waived by this potential victim.

As it became obvious to the road crew that their fellow worker was about to be flattened on the roadside by an angry mob of motorists, they dropped their picks and shovels and ran to his aid. There was a battle about to break out and *my car* was on the front line. Since I had been the first car to stop, and only inches from the old man, it seemed this was all happening right in my lap.

I'm the type of person who avoids violence and conflict whenever possible. If there is a movie with violent scenes, I have to cover my eyes to avoid seeing the bloodshed. I found myself surrounded by all this anger so I turned to God for help; remembering what I had been writing and teaching to others.

I focused on the *Christ Light of God Perfection* in each man around my car. Since it hadn't occurred to me until now to be angry, it was easier for any judgment of either side to be released. The focus was one of gratitude that no one was injured. I chose to see only Christed souls even if they were about ready to hit one another. I put my hand up and sent out peace and love. The face of the master Jesus was pictured over each man's face replacing the angry faces. Instantly the fists turned to open hands. The cursing and angry words were silenced. The expressions on the faces of the men went from fierceness to stunned confusion. They peacefully and quietly turned in the opposite direction and went back to their cars.

The work crew, who had dropped their shovels and run to protect the old man from the angry crowd, also turned and went back to their work. The man who I had spoken to who had been holding the old man up by his collar, ready to bury his fist in his face, at that same instant, let go of his grip. He dropped his arms, opened his fists, and calmly walked back to his vehicle. The old man stepped aside and we continued to drive down the road.

There was absolutely no doubt in my mind after this of the power of the Christ light – the power of love. It only takes one heart based in love to stop an army of angry aggressors. One candle in the night can light a whole room.

I haven't exaggerated any of this story. It is still difficult for part of me to believe that no one was hurt and nothing was damaged, and in the end, all were immersed in love. I must have been an emissary of peace before I knew what that was because this happened before meeting James Twyman. The following poem sums it all up:

The only true reflection of God is Love.
Love is all there is.

In this silent moment,
Remembering all that is.
I ponder life's true purpose,
Rekindle myths that trick.

Above us and below us,
The truth is all around.
Beckoning with simplicity.
Love is all we've found.

Hatred promises righteousness,
And fear – insecurity.
Protecting self from these,
Becomes necessity.

Our burdens we've created,
Of emotion gone insane.
Replace them now with God's love,
As our purpose we reclaim.

When we look into the mirror,
The reflection tells it all.
What do you see as you gaze,
A God of love or war?

I was reminded by a friend after she heard the story of the old man with the rag, to focus on remembering the Christ in every cell of the body. It was simple, not something I hadn't heard before. In fact I've said those very words to many others.

In the story, the focus was on being the channel for the Christ Light and projecting it to everything around me. This focus of love defused the fear and anger that surrounded my car. If you were to see the car as an extension of one's self, a whole new purpose for what happened would unfold.

Within each of us is a spark of love – the essence of God. Sometimes it is locked deep within our heart, covered up and surrounded by fear, anger, self-judgment, and conflict. Over the years and many lifetimes, the illusion of separateness has put up walls of protection that we believe shield our light from being attacked. We think the light is vulnerable because it is surrounded by fear.

What if fear didn't really exist? What if it was created because of a false belief of separateness from God? Would this light be all that remained? Do the walls of protection actually imprison the light with what appears real and yet is an illusionary barrier that contains it and keeps it from coming to the surface?

My friend was reminding me that the barriers are self-inflicted. We wear them like a turtle wears a shell. (Like Mike wore his t-shirt.) Like the turtle, when we are feeling brave, we poke our heads out to see what is real. If we look in the mirror and we see fear, conflict, or rejection all around us, we quickly pull our heads back into this illusionary shell of protection. It is in that moment that we must remember the truth – love is all there is. Then the illusion is not reflected back; it simply disappears. It never existed.

For a brief moment in my car every cell of my body remembered the light that it has always been. Remembering the truth those many years ago, I had acted to affect the mirror of love all around me. In this state of being – Christ Consciousness – I only saw love. The angry crowd had disappeared.

This turtle has climbed back into her shell and forgotten her true purpose for being on this planet. She forgot that every thread of the Universal Tapestry was Love.

The focus now is to shed this heavy burdensome shell that no longer serves and step fully into a new vehicle; a light vehicle. As we drive down the road, the mirror all around shall be the one true reality – love. When each of us is successful in doing this in every moment, our planet and all creation will have ascended, and the Universal Tapestry of Love will have been woven.

Behold

Behold – I am one.

Behold – I am peace.

Behold – I am eternal.

One peace eternal.

Behold – I am one.

Behold – I am light.

Behold – I am love.

One light – love.

Behold, I am one peace eternal, one light, love.

BEHOLD – I AM

Chapter 19

It is three in the morning and I am wide awake. Words are streaming through my head and there seems no choice but to get up and go down stairs to write. One would think by now I would be accustomed to this. As I lay in bed arguing with myself a part of me knows that in the end the other part will give in and once more the pages I write will flow.

This morning one story is *demanding* to be written. The purpose of this book could be summed up in just this story.

It all started one morning when I stopped in for a cup of coffee at my friend Sandy's house. After dropping the boys off for school, I would occasionally visit with her. We were both focused on paying our bills and finding employment that would get us through. I had just returned to Virginia and completed the construction of our new home, when the illusion of lack reared its ugly head once more. It had been years since I had this awful feeling of not being supported by the Universe. The faith that had sustained me since Pete had departed, and the belief that whatever we needed would be given to us, had faded. Faith and belief had been clouded by doubt and fear. I found myself once again staring the illusion of poverty square in the face. This couldn't be happening. I had already resolved that one.

I had forgotten one universal rule. When you say to yourself,

"I don't have to worry about that anymore. I've licked that problem.", you'd better duck. It's just about to come back and this time catch you off-guard because you weren't expecting it. The lesson is always there for us to experience and to learn from the next level. The way *we choose* to deal with it is what changes.

Poverty consciousness was deeply rooted in me, as a tool I had been given by the Universe at birth – my teacher. One may learn a powerful lesson when one recognizes that poverty consciousness is not a burden but a gift. If God is everything, then God is also our boss – the source of everything in our world; all money and possessions. Every time fear clouds the truth, poverty stands waiting. One could say fear and poverty walk hand in hand with doubt and disbelief. It was time to once again turn fear to faith and poverty to unlimited support.

My friend Sandy and I were having a similar conversation when she said, "I've been offered a job but it is not something I want to do. A friend of mine told me about someone who needs help. This woman's mother is ill and in need of round the clock nursing care. She is having difficulty finding people to care for her. Joyce, would you be interested in the job?" The illusion of lack had drawn me in so far that it wouldn't have mattered what job she was offering, I would have taken it.

Still I hesitated. I'd never done any nursing. Was this something I was qualified to do? I started to listen again, pulling myself out of fear and beginning the creative process of trusting my guidance and listening to Spirit. I was waking up to the illusion in the moment and having faith that the opportunity being given to me was perfect no matter how inappropriate it may have seemed. In this case the guidance proved to be a real blessing. I cast away all my fears and doubts, trusted that the Universe had, through Sandy, sent the perfect job.

I went to meet Georgia. It was clear she needed help. Phyllis, her mother, had just come home from the hospital. Georgia was also taking care of her son, Michael, who was in a wheelchair and also required round-the-clock care.

We communicated easily and Georgia took me to meet Phyllis. I liked both of them and wanted to do what I could to be of service and at the same time work my way out of debt. There was a strong inner knowing that I was to take this job even though I had never cared for anyone in this way. Georgia knew I was a Reiki Master and had done guided visualizations, and regressions. She was open and interested in my skills and thought it might be of help to her mother. She explained that nursing experience was not a requirement for the job. I decided to accept the offer.

Phyllis was to help me fine-tune another healing tool that I possessed. I had noticed that when I worked for her, I would take on symptoms of the same ailment and feel as she did. This is called being an empath. I could tell what Phyllis was feeling even when I wasn't there with her, experiencing the same symptoms and physical problems she was experiencing. I was aware of what was happening but didn't understand why I wasn't able to clear her energy from my physical being so I wouldn't become ill. Was I losing my identity and taking on someone else's? Had I done this before? Of course I had, especially when opening my heart to a man. In relationships, I had a tendency to give too much because I cared. I would lose myself and become whoever that person I cared for needed.

I did care for Phyllis. We were completely different on the surface but underneath, I had a feeling we had much in common. This hadn't been logically explained, yet there was just a knowing that by helping her, I was helping myself too.

As she got stronger, so did I and a unique friendship developed. Some parts of the tapestry were getting clearer, but Phyllis's eyesight was not. She was having difficulty seeing and asked if I would help her finish her next book, *Rainbows In The Mist,* by reading her notes as she typed what I read. I had no trouble reading her writing and we worked well together.

When I went to work for Phyllis Whitney, her name didn't mean anything to me. I was just going to help a friend and earn some much needed money. The only books I had been interested in were non-fiction or spiritually oriented. Mystery novels were not my cup of tea. How was I to know that Phyllis was a famous mystery writer? She had just finished book number seventy-four when I started writing this book. She started seventy-five before seventy-four was in print. It was to be the story of her life. What a coincidence; we were both working on similar projects. Imagine that.

Phyllis was feeling better and her eyesight was returning in one eye after successful surgery. She no longer needed round-the-clock care but she kept me on part-time – just a few hours a week. I wasn't sure why I was still there but I kept getting the message to stay. I enjoyed our time together.

Knowing that I was a writer, she gave me part of her new book to read. She had started writing it but had to stop. I loved what I read and realized I was in writing school, seeing firsthand how a professional organized a book. I learned new skills and found a new purpose for being there.

A deeper understanding grew as I read of her early childhood. I discovered why I felt we had something in common when on the surface we seemed so totally opposite. I felt honored to be there with her and very appreciative of the opportunity to learn from a master.

The time came when it became difficult for her to sit at a typewriter. Remembering that I had been able to read her writing, she asked me if I would like some extra work. It was arranged that I pick up her handwritten manuscript, take it home, and put it on my computer, bringing the copies back to her for editing and rewriting.

Many prayers were answered by having faith in the guidance that I received to go and help a friend. I was working at home, learning, and writing all at the same time. The universe had sent the best possible teacher. All I had to do was listen.

Somehow Phyllis seemed to know exactly what I needed to learn. When I was worried about whether my book would be published, she wrote about how many rejections slips she had gotten. When I started to question why I must write and toyed with the idea of getting a *real job*, she gave me this advice, "Write because it is what you have to do, not because you think you will profit." What faith! When I was feeling lost and without direction, she wrote tips on how to organize and outline a novel. I never shared with her what was happening, but somehow what she wrote was just what I needed to learn for the next step.

I am so glad I listened to my inner voice. I have new friends and a wonderful learning opportunity. My focus is no longer on fear and lack but on creativity and abundance.

Chapter 20

It is Christmas Eve and I have awakened early once more with a poem echoing in my ears. I am being told this is a Christmas present from Spirit to me. Further instructions reveal that I am to give this present to all the members of a small church that I attend. This church was having a candlelight service that evening.

The plan was to make copies and give each person a print of the poem, but then Mike tells me that the printer is down. If I am to give the poem, then it would have to be read out loud to a packed room full of people, half of whom were strangers. I argued with Spirit for a while about doing this.

We decided to turn it over to the universe. If the pastor, my friend Mary, will allow this last minute change in the program, I would recite the poem and if she wouldn't, then I was in luck.

So I went to the candlelight service and approached Mary, "I've been given a gift and asked by Spirit to share it with everyone. May I read it tonight?"

She sat quietly for a moment and said, "I'll meditate about it." A few minutes later Mary called me over and said, "You may read it following the offering since it is a gift."

I resigned myself to this fate and nervously sat down to await my time to give this gift. When it was time I went up to the front. I was surprised with the ease at which I recited this poem:

A Present From God

It's Christmas Eve in the morning.
Echoing in my ears are many Christmas carols,
Sung by angels we have heard on high,
Sweetly singing lullabies,
Hark the Yuletide in the sky.
Peace on earth, this is their cry.

On wings of eagles fly they now,
Unto eternity the winds shall blow,
Sounds of joy forever bold.
On waves of love God's songs are heard.
Till every creature has embraced
The Mind of Christ that is its fate.

Not fate of anger, fear, or woe,
But fate of God's eternal grace.
Wrapped with love and a golden bow,
This present now our gift shall be,
When we receive eternal peace.
God's holy instant forever be.

As we give birth to this new year,
Let there be peace in every ear.
And every heart embrace God's love,
With knowing we have always been ONE.
So Hark! The herald angels sing –
Glory to this new born ONE.

Near the end I raised my hands to the sky as I dramatically said the last two lines, *"So Hark! The herald angels sing – Glory to this new born ONE."*

Returning to my seat I was relieved. Everything had gone well and it was over. Then Mary said, "Now turn to your programs, which I hadn't had time to look at yet. We will now sing – *Hark The Herald Angels Sing*." Mary looked at me and I at her. We were both surprised – what a coincidence. The entire congregation was impressed at the perfect timing and we hadn't planned any of it. Spirit must have known all along that this hymn would follow the reading of the gift. It has been included in this book as a gift to you.

It's Christmas Day and what a wonderful day it has been full of unexpected events and first time experiences. I was at the last minute invited to spend the holiday with Betty in Washington, D.C. For some reason she came back to a cold Virginia leaving beautiful sunny Hawaii behind. She was staying with two other friends, Connie and Joy. I hadn't seen any of them for quite some time and had missed them.

When Betty called I quickly changed my plans for the day and accepted their dinner invitation. I had expected to spend Christmas with Mike and Jon but the boys had plans for the day with their friends. They were becoming more independent – growing up. This was to be my first Christmas without them. If I stayed at home I would have been alone most of the day.

After I decided to go to D.C., I called my brother and mother. It seemed only natural to visit them also since they were only an hour away from where I had been invited for dinner. We had planned for all of them to come to Virginia a few days after Christmas. They didn't mind the last minute change; in fact it seemed better for them too.

Because of the decision to be with family and close friends on Christmas Day, the boys and I opened our presents on Christmas Eve, another first. We usually did this Christmas morning. Jon didn't come home from his job until after midnight so technically it was morning. Mike was glad to get up even though he was already in bed if it meant opening presents early. So we had our joy of giving and the boys – now young men – could sleep in the next morning. Jon offered to take Mike to his friend's house. This made it possible for me to leave before they got up. It usually took about three and a half hours to drive to my brother's house.

The drive to Washington was peaceful, as there were few cars on the road. As I drove, through the small towns in Virginia and then the cities near D.C. and then in Maryland, I imagined all the families gathered together to celebrate the holiday in their own way. Images of little ones waking up at dawn and dragging their blurry eyed-parents out of their warm beds filled my mind. I felt a bit lonely and sad. My first Christmas day without my children. When had they grown up? The baby quilts had long ago been woven into the tapestry and it seemed like only yesterday that Christmas meant Santa coming down the chimney. Now all that seemed left were the memories and a few old snapshots of the boys perched on Santa's knee and a home video of the past year.

Memories seemed to be all that I had in my car along with packages I would be delivering this holiday. Had I forgotten the true meaning of this day? As it turned out, my sleigh held much more than emptiness and I was to become my own Santa bringing the gift of love to everyone including myself.

Every other year at this time, Jon, Mike, and I would have been sitting under our live tree decorated with memories of Christmas past, a tapestry of its own, with popcorn strung and hung from branches that struggled to hold up under the weight of all the ornaments and lights. All those years I had resisted the notion of an artificial tree. This year when I asked the boys if we should get a tree, they said no. They really didn't care whether we had one or not. For the first time I decided not to bother, instead I decorated our rather large gardenia which was in bloom with tiny ornaments and lights. Jon helped me put a garland around the archway in the center of the house and this also was also illuminated. We decided that our whole house was the tree; after all it was made of wood, so we decorated it. The boys liked this idea because they said we weren't killing a tree. The gardenia seemed to love the attention it was getting and continued to bloom through the holiday.

My brother Wayne and his wife Angel had just moved into a beautiful new home and this was to be a first for them too. As I pulled up to the house, I put on a funny, fake pair of red antlers and a large sleigh bell around my neck. My brother and I liked to play tricks on each other and joke a lot. Our family has a good sense of humor and I knew this would be a lot of fun for everyone. Maybe instead of antlers I was really putting on a mask so that they wouldn't see my tears. With arms full of packages and looking rather ridiculous, I entered my brother's very impressive home and was received with great joy and laughter.

They had created an enchanted space which was decorated traditionally. The whole family of about twelve was gathered. There were children, and babies, and a huge, beautiful tree full of all of the memories of years gone by; with popcorn and candy and stockings hung by the fireplace. Presents were everywhere and so was great joy. My sadness became a memory as I settled into the moment to create a very special day with a much loved family.

When the University of Science and Philosophy moved many alumni and volunteers were each given the gift of a case of books at a Christmas banquet. The books were found in a closet on the third floor, just before their move from the Palace at Swannanoa. The book was written by Lao Russell and titled, "Love." Spirit instructed me to set out on the table many copies of this book and give it as a present to anyone in my family who wanted to take one.

In the past I hadn't shared much about my spiritual life because I feared rejection, so I was a little reluctant to do this. Part of me knew today was the day to come out of the closet and take off the mask that I wore when I was with my family. To my surprise, our mother, who is an avid reader, picked the book up first and read out loud to the whole family. She opened it to the most meaningful passage and read, "Love is the most powerful force in the universe." She then continued to read many other passages and seemed impressed with the book. Was this *my* mother who I thought only read mysteries and romance novels and didn't want to hear the word 'spiritual'?

The door was open and the stage was set. Before I knew it,

the poem I had written on Christmas Eve and read at church was in my hand and I was now very nervously reading it to my whole family. This time it was much more difficult to deliver. I felt naked, having taken off all of my masks, even the antlers. I was so glad when it was finally over. To my surprise everyone loved it and they loved the real me!

As I was leaving, Wayne helped me put my things in the car. Through the window as I sat behind the wheel, he thanked me again for the present of my poem and the book. It was then that I broke down and cried because I felt so loved.

It was time to go to be with my spiritual family, Connie, Betty and Joy. So I put on my antlers again but this time it was just for fun, not a cover-up. We had a wonderful turkey dinner with all the trimmings and exchanged small presents as tokens of love. I told them what had happened with my family. Sharing this great gift of acceptance with them I read the same poem. Reading it was easier the third time.

Then in my ear Spirit said to me, "Read what you wrote this morning too." No one had yet heard these words. And I was then instructed that they were to be the last pages of this book. I tried several times just to read the first sentences and couldn't stop crying, having to start over and over. My friends came and held me as I let go of all of the pain and emotion that had been buried so deep and covered up for many years. My heart was being healed by love and as the tears were wiped with care from my face, I started once more and read the following words....

December 25, 1997 – 5 a.m.

We started our journey together at the beginning of this year. Now it is Christmas Day – how appropriate. This book began with the story of Pete's passing and now these last pages are to be written on his birthday. Yes, my husband's birthday was on December 25, 1946. He is 51 today if we were to consider linear time but to Pete, that no longer exists. He exists in a world that is right here and now, but is in the moment invisible to us. Pete is in a place where there is no time and indeed no physical space. His presence can be felt as his spirit lay next to me. At the same moment, his consciousness is soaring in space at the heart of the cosmos – in the heart of God.

Pete has given me the greatest present I have ever received. That present is my new awareness. That present is who I am. That present is the journey we have just shared in the pages of this tapestry. Without his journey and sacrifice, this new awareness would not have been possible.

Thank you Pete for helping me to see and be a little closer to the truth. Thank you for sharing your heart that now beats as one and resides with Source, as well as with mine. Thank you for teaching me by example how to be *present,* living only in the moment.

As we stand on the brink of a new year and a new millennium, it is already done. We are like you Pete, already home. For in the heart of God, our hearts abide. As we see through the eyes of our soul, we remember – we are all one. The truth is we were never separate; we have always been united. With no place to go and no time to get there; take a deep breath and in the stillness, embrace all that there is around you – LOVE.

LOVE IS ALL THERE IS

Afterward

New Tapestry – Phoenix

Who are we? Are we our physical bodies? Are we our minds? Are we our possessions? Are we our personal view of reality or the dreams that we create? When we make our transition (die of the flesh), what remains where we once held a space in time? Our physical bodies turn to dust eventually and our minds joyfully exit the dream, returning to their original state. The dream that we created while a part of the collective creation melts. What is left is who we are.

Are we nothing? We are but we are not. If we were nothing, we could not create the dream. We could not participate in the collective mind. I suggest that what remains is life force. Taoist call this life force Chi.

I have come to believe that everything in creation is a dream created by our minds because of beliefs that have been programmed and handed down from one generation to the next – from womb to womb. As babies, we are pure consciousness, and have not been conditioned by the collective mind with all its beliefs and limiting views of who we are. The collective mind holds the program that we are our bodies, our minds, our beliefs; and works to keep us asleep in the dream, believing that the dream is who we are.

When we are small children, we play and we are happy. We have not been taught in the beginning that we are bad. Innocence doesn't know the meaning of the word 'judgment' yet. We are quickly conditioned, as were our parents, to judge ourselves, and then to project that judgment onto others. This is the beginning of a deep sleep within the collective dream. We become dreamers not knowing we are asleep, thinking that our life is all there is. At pivotal points in the dream state, we are presented with opportunities to awaken. Many of these opportunities appear to be nightmares while in reality they are our gifts.

When you have a nightmare as a small child, the fear causes you to wake up. Some sudden occurrence in the dream shakes your consciousness and you are no longer asleep in the dream. You cry out for help and mom or dad come to comfort you and tell you that it was just a bad dream. They tell you not to be afraid. It was all just an illusion they say. They assure you that there is nothing to fear but fear itself. So you believe what they say and go back to sleep. This time, in your dream, you create fun and enjoy the dream. While dreaming again you forget that it is just a dream.

I thought that this book was complete in December of 1997 and did my best to get it published. Obviously that didn't happen then and it was put aside as my busy dream continued to weave itself. Knowing that there is always a reason and that I have always been ahead of when I believed things should be happening, I trusted that all was as it should be for the highest good of all.

On March 1, 2002, disaster struck. My house and everything from the past turned to ashes. The nightmare that was responsible for awakening me from a deep sleep was our house burning to the ground. In what seemed a moment, all of who I believed I was became ashes. As anyone who has gone through such loss can attest, I was dazed and lost. Almost immediately something happened. I awoke in a theater that was ablaze. I had no choice but to run out of the theater and slam the door behind me.

Since then, every day I thank the nightmare for waking me up. I thank the fire for clearing the clutter that I had created around me. I had become a slave to my possessions. They owned me. The dream had consumed me. I had lost the innocence and joy that I once had as a small child before nightmares had been created by my consciousness. I had lost the freedom that we found living in the moment in the motor home – consciously intending and creating every day. Fear and judgment had clouded my vision and created separation. I no longer loved myself so I didn't feel worthy of having a peaceful, loving existence in the dream. I realized I had been creating dramas that I *must* overcome in order to prove that I was worthy. I was caught in a vicious downward spiral that had finally hit rock bottom. Suddenly I was free to soar in my spirit. Now there was only one direction to go in and that was up. Up was out of the dream, out of the theater of creation.

This book is the story of the dream-state in which we all find ourselves. It is a story of never-ending dramas and how you may choose to awaken within the dream and become a conscious co-creator. It is intended to be the story of how to claim conscious presence.

Presence

To seek love is to look outside self for identity.
What we seek in love is consciousness.
We ask for love and get the opposite.
We ask for love and get the drug of choice –
Loss, rejection, humiliation, control, judgment.
We ask for love and get hooked into the suffering wheel of karma –
receiving our fix.

Upon awakening and surrendering, the drug of love is discovered.
Now we find our consciousness seated in the theater of Creation,
Watching the stories, the projections, the fragments of the soul,
and the mind.
We remember that this is what we created love to be.

Awakened now and leaving the theater, all that remains is
Our consciousness outside of Creation – presence – energy – Chi.
Consciousness existed before we created the love of our choice.
Love was the play, the story, the drug –
Our creation within the creation.
Creation within the dream.

When one chooses to claim consciousness outside of creation,
One is making a conscious choice to unify, to awaken,

To be Present

While editing this book in August of 2011, I found this email which I sent after the fire. Reading it reminded me of all the gifts I was given as a result of our house burning to the ground. It is my belief that we are on the brink of a quantum opportunity for growth, as we near 2012. Many people identify with what will be ending, as changes of the future become more obvious. I choose to identify with what is being born, for out of the ashes will rise the new tapestry of Creation, the Phoenix. The following message puts the final threads of completion into the weave of this creation, giving birth to a new tapestry.....

It is a cold January 26th of 2003. The sun has just risen in a blazing gold and pink. A beautiful backdrop of the mountains surrounds the little cottage in which I now live with my son Mike and Mickey Blue Eyes, our new cat.

Last year was full of bittersweet challenges and great opportunities. This year I have chosen to be the cougar and reclaim my personal power in the NOW. I am full of hope as I write these words, but there is also a little fear that creeps in from moment-to-moment. It is that little bit of fear, that at times, makes me wonder if I am just some nut case ready for an institution.

I have always been aware that in this world we created, where our consciousness resides, there is a fine line between genius and insanity. Is that because the closer we get to the real truth, the more we realize how insanely the world we have created has evolved? Or, is it because the mind creates the insanity? Maybe insanity doesn't exist and genius is just an illusion created by the mind to make it feel important. Just thinking about it could make one a little crazy.

Residing in the mind alone is not a happy place to be. The mind is a wonderful tool, but when it is in league with the will or negative ego, it can be a real downer. This year, I have chosen to find the balance between the mind, the will and the heart. In finding that balance, I have noticed that imbalance has to be created. By experiencing what isn't desired, what is sought after is defined. To find peace, chaos was created. To find joy, pain was experienced. To find love, fears and separation surround us.

The backdrop never changes. The mountains stay fixed, as the eternal sun rises to shine its golden light, on the consciousness of our creation. What we may change, is our ability to drink in that golden light in a state of peace, joy and eternal love.

About the Author

Joyce is passionate about sharing heart resonate frequencies with her voice and healing practice. She holds a BFA degree in sculpture from the Maryland Institute College of Art. She taught art for fifteen years. Other earlier professions include textile designer and protective clothing designer for the US Department of Defense. After the tragic death of her husband in a plane crash in 1983, Joyce was propelled into deep spiritual studies. As a result of this quantum opportunity for growth she became a regression therapist. The new connection to her husband's soul in the spirit realms gave her a different awareness and understanding of the Universal Soul. As a trance channel, she has assisted many in spiritual counseling sessions communicating with loved ones on the other side of the veil.

She also uses medical intuitive, quantum healing, and physic surgery techniques. Joyce combines all that she has gathered in over thirty years of study in her private consultations, acting as a conduit for heart resonate light, assisting souls to free themselves of programing that no longer supports them. Working at the cellular DNA level, these old beliefs may be reprogrammed, shifting recurring patterns.

Joyce is a certified International Sound Healer. She has studied with Jonathan Goldman, Tom Kenyon, Tashu Lama, and Tashi Lama who was the Dali Lama's Chant Master. She has recorded two CDs of live improvisational concerts. Each song on these CDs was created in the moment, singing the frequencies of the soul's that were present. Some of the songs were recorded at the historic Roslyn Chapel in Scotland. By going to joycegedeon.com you can hear three of the songs as well as listen to live channeling sessions. Over 100 poems are also on this free site.

www.ingramcontent.com/pod-product-compliance
Lightning Source LLC
Chambersburg PA
CBHW060244290526
45789CB00001B/179